DATA-DRIVEN PRINT

PRINTING INDUSTRY CENTER SERIES

DATA-DRIVEN PRINT

STRATEGY AND IMPLEMENTATION

PATRICIA SORCE

MICHAEL PLETKA

RIT CARY GRAPHIC ARTS PRESS
ROCHESTER, NY

Data-Driven Print: Strategy and Implementation
Patricia Sorce, Michael Pletka
Printing Industry Center Series: 2

Published and distributed by
RIT Cary Graphic Arts Press
90 Lomb Memorial Drive
Rochester, New York 14623-5604
http://library.rit.edu/cary/carypress.html

Printed in the United States by Thomson-Shore, Inc.
ISBN-13: 978-1-933360-06-5
ISBN-10: 1-933360-06-2

Designed by Marnie Soom / RIT Cary Graphic Arts Press
Typeface: Whitney by Tobias Frere-Jones / Hoefler & Frere-Jones
Excerpts reprinted by permission of *DM News, Digital Output,* and PIA/GATF.

Library of Congress Cataloging-in-Publication Data

Sorce, Patricia.
Data-driven print : strategy and implementation / Patricia Sorce, Michael Pletka.
p. cm. — (Printing industry center series ; 2)
Includes bibliographical references and index.
ISBN-13: 978-1-933360-06-5 (alk. paper)
ISBN-10: 1-933360-06-2 (alk. paper)
1. Advertising, Direct-mail. 2. Digital printing. I. Pletka, Michael. II. Title.
III. Series.
HF5861.S67 2006
659.13'3—dc22

2005037422

CONTENTS

LIST OF FIGURES

LIST OF TABLES

ABOUT THE AUTHORS

Patricia Sorce is currently co-director of the Printing Industry Center at RIT and administrative chair of the RIT School of Print Media. She teaches in the areas of marketing research, buyer behavior, and database marketing. Her current research is focused on the topics of relationship marketing and the factors that impact the demand for data-driven print.

She earned a Ph.D. in cognitive psychology from the University of Massachusetts. She has published in refereed marketing, management, and psychology journals. These publications have spanned a wide range of topics including basic research in psychology, marketing segmentation analysis, and most recently, Internet buying behavior and relationship marketing. Before her appointment as co-director of the Printing Industry Center, she served as associate dean of the College of Business from 1996 through 2001. She has been on the faculty of the RIT College of Business for over 20 years.

Michael Pletka is currently manager, customer business development, Xerox Production Systems Group. In this role, he manages ProfitQuick, a financial modeling tool used worldwide by sales and print providers to help them understand the financial implications of investing in digital technology. Michael often meets with graphic communications establishments to discuss the considerations and opportunities of creating a digital business. He also has experience in digital print production, and is knowledgeable in cost estimation, variable data printing and workflow. Michael received a Bachelor of Science in Printing Management and an MBA from Rochester Institute of Technology. He was a Printing Industry Center Research Scholar during his graduate program, focused in the areas of digital business models and the opportunities in variable data printing.

PREFACE

MUCH OF THE CONTENT FOR THIS BOOK came from research conducted by the Printing Industry Center at the Rochester Institute of Technology (RIT), investigating factors that impact the proliferation of digital color printing technology. The Printing Industry Center at RIT is dedicated to the study of major business environment influences in the printing industry brought on by new technologies and societal change, and has undertaken a number of research initiatives to investigate these issues. RIT was selected by the Alfred P. Sloan Foundation in 2001 to host a Sloan Industry Center. The resulting Printing Industry Center is a joint program of the RIT School of Print Media and RIT's College of Business, emphasizing Sloan's long-standing tradition of applying a broad multidisciplinary approach to industry investigations and findings.

We have compiled this book with three audiences in mind. For print services providers, we address this question: "Should my business invest in digital printing technology in order to create data-driven communications that result in personalized or customized printed materials?" This book answers the question of how to overcome the strategic and operational barriers that have impeded the growth of this media form. In these pages, we will document the current use of personalization and custom communication in the U.S. in the early 21st century, and identify the best practices, best prospects, and associated business models for delivering value to printing clients.

For print media consultants who work within a corporate communications department or in an advertising agency, we will discuss when customized marketing communications pay off, describe creative options for data-driven communications, and identify the infrastructure requirements needed to deliver such programs.

Our final audience is academic. Students and faculty will find this book a concise supplemental text for courses in direct marketing and database publishing.

ACKNOWLEDGMENTS

THE AUTHORS ARE DEEPLY INDEBTED TO Barbara Pellow for her leadership in this research program while she was at the Rochester Institute of Technology. Barb served as a mentor to Michael during his undergraduate and graduate education and as a wonderful colleague to Pat as Co-Director of the Printing Industry Center at RIT. Barb's extensive contacts within the printing industry and her insightful cases studies of the barriers to adopting digital color printing provided much of the impetus for the work reported in this book. We owe her a great deal.

This work was supported by a grant from the Alfred P. Sloan Foundation Industries Studies Program. We want to thank Gail Pesyna and Frank Mayadas, program directors for the Sloan Foundation, for their support in sustaining the Printing Industry Center at RIT. The Printing Industry Center is also supported by grants from industry. We would like to thank the following firms for their generous support: Adobe Systems Incorporated, Baldwin Technology Company, Inc., Creo Inc., Eastman Kodak Company, Heidelberg, Hewlett Packard, IBM Printing Systems, MeadWestvaco Corporation, NPES, RR Donnelley, Standard Register, the U.S. Government Printing Office, Vertis, VIGC, Weyerhaeuser, and Xerox Corporation.

Many students worked on the Printing Industry Center research program while they were completing their graduate programs at RIT. We want to thank Brett Daly, Heather Banis, Lauren Olson, Katie Moore, and Svetlana Kirpichenko for their contributions to this research. Thanks also to Franziska Frey, assistant professor in the RIT School of Print Media, who co-authored some of the original research contributing to this book, and helped in supervising many of these students during their thesis research.

We also want to thank the people and publications who provided case studies included in this book: Sandra Rothenberg, associate professor in the RIT College of Business; Frank Cost, associate dean and professor in the RIT College of Imaging Arts and Sciences and co-director of the Printing Industry Center at RIT; Steve Couture, senior manager of Strategic Marketing at Standard Register; Lisa Boyer, president of Lexinet; John Hawkes, editor of *Menu* magazine, Wegmans; Cary Sherburne, senior editor at WhatTheyThink, in cooperation with the PIA/GATF Digital Print Council; *Digital Output Magazine*; and *DM News.*

We are also indebted to those who provided insightful feedback and commentary on earlier drafts of this book: Keith M. Nickoloff, president of PathForward; Robert G. Wagner, vice president / general manager, Creative Services Business, Worldwide Graphic Communications Industry Business at Xerox Production Systems Group; Julie W. McEwan, Public Relations at Standard Register; Stanley M. Widrick, professor of marketing, College of Business at RIT; Cary Sherburne, senior editor at WhatTheyThink, and Frank Romano, professor emeritus, RIT.

Adrienne McHargue, Communications Director of the Printing Industry Center at RIT, was instrumental in all phases of this project from data collection through editing and production. Thanks also to Patricia Cost who provided her editing magic to make the manuscript as readable as it is. We could not have done it without you both.

Lastly, we want to thank Joan Stone, dean of the College of Imaging Arts and Sciences, and Frank Cost, associate dean of the College of Imaging Arts and Sciences, professor, and co-director of the Printing Industry Center for their personal and professional support to the authors. Without their leadership, vision, and day-to-day involvement, the Printing Industry Center at RIT would not exist.

CHAPTER ONE

THE POWER OF PERSONALIZATION

WE HAVE ALL EXPERIENCED IT. In a crowded room filled with party chatter, you can concentrate on your own conversation with two colleagues and, without too much trouble, ignore what is going on around you. Then a voice within earshot, coming from a conversation in another corner of the room, mentions your name. Your attention, and maybe your head, turns to the other conversation. Even though your name is not shouted or even called out, your attention moves away from your own companions and toward the other conversation. Rude behavior on your part, yes, but it is almost impossible for you to resist this distraction.

The ability to focus on one perceptual stimulus among many is called *selective attention*, and has been a mainstay of the study of cognitive psychology since the 1960s.[1] If we think of all the information that comes in through our senses at any given moment, we realize that it would overwhelm us if we weren't able to focus on one input stream at a time. Selecting one particular input stream enables us to pay close attention to what is happening in that stream. When some powerful, compelling input arrives in a different stream, it interrupts our attention long enough for us to analyze whether we want to turn to it. A name has this power to interrupt and grab our attention away from what we're doing. Other pertinent stimuli can distract us as well. For horse lovers, for example, a mention of the Kentucky Derby or a particular breed of horses will turn heads.

How can marketers harness the attention-grabbing power of a customer's name or some other personal information in an advertising message? First we need to define what we mean by *personalizing* an advertising message. Personal names are actually not necessary. InfoTrends/CAP Ventures, a graphic media consulting firm, defines the term *personalized communication* as a customized offer based on stored preferences, needs, or potential value of a customer.[2] Zahay and Griffin recognize the two-way intention of the communication, and define personalized communication as "a specialized flow of interactive communication between parties."[3] In fact, several related terms have been coined around the concept of personalized communication, most notably customized communications and variable data printing (VDP). We will coin the term data-driven print to describe the means of production that results in customized text and graphics in printed materials. Data-driven print is the means to the end of creating relevant, often content-rich, customized marketing communications.

The use of customized marketing communication is determined by the marketing goals of a firm. To ensure an effective marketing program, a product or service offering should be integrated and consistent with its promotion, pricing, and distribution elements.[4] Such marketing mixes are usually offered to a clearly defined set of customers. This segmentation and targeting of groups of customers is the cornerstone of marketing strategy. Customizing a marketing program to a single customer is at the extreme end of the targeting continuum.

Customized products range from the creation of a single object for a customer, like a made-to-measure business suit, to the mass customization now seen in manufacturing.[5] An example of mass customization is the Dell Web site that allows a user to configure a new PC and determine how much it will cost. Sophisticated information technology at the point of purchase facilitates order entry, enables individual customers to design their own products, and gives them a choice of manufacturing and delivery options, all accomplished as simply as traditional mass production. Customized communication is an important intermediate step in achieving the end goal of configuring a unique product for an individual consumer, many consumers at a time.

Customized marketing communications can be supported by other business models in addition to the build-to-order model described above. Direct marketers have pioneered the use of mailing lists of customers who share at least one thing in common. For example, the subscription list of *Vintage Guitar* magazine can help identify prospective customers who already have an interest in historical musical instruments. Today's direct marketing activities still use the U.S. postal system extensively to reach consumers, but the ability to customize printed communications has made direct mail campaigns more focused. Just as Internet technology has allowed businesses to customize the online shopping experience, digital printing technology has enabled firms to create colorful, personalized, and more relevant printed marketing communications. Digital printing is any form of printing where a digital data stream, and not a physical master such as a plate, is used to determine the rendering of the printed image. It is therefore possible to print a unique image on each successive page.

CUSTOMIZED MARKETING COMMUNICATIONS

The term *customized marketing communications* refers to the entire complex range of marketing materials that can be designed using descriptive and behavioral information about individual customers and delivered through a variety of media channels. The customized message can be as simple as a specific name and address on a postal mailing or as complex as a unique promotional offer based on prior purchase history presented at the point of purchase.

Customized marketing communications are data-driven. Data about individuals are collected, and then specific information is delivered back to those individuals through direct or interactive marketing channels (media). The decision to use either direct marketing (through postal mail or email) or interactive marketing (through a commercial Web site, interactive TV, or a hand-held mobile device) is made as part of a broader integrated communications plan that can utilize a variety of media to achieve its marketing goals.

Much of the excitement about customized marketing communications has centered on the Internet as the primary delivery medium,[6] through the use of customized Web pages or customized emails. However, consumer reactions to customized marketing communications in the electronic or interactive world have been mixed. In a recent survey, business customers evaluated the importance of a variety of Web site functions. Being recognized as a return visitor to a Web site was rated less important than the ability to customize content or configure products.[7] In other words, users felt that being able to customize a product or interact with a Web site was more valuable than being recognized by the site. Other research has shown that when customers had the opportunity to customize a Web page or portal, the majority have not done so.[8]

There is an even stronger ambivalence regarding email marketing. Because of concerns about spam, advertisers are less likely to increase their use of email marketing, where the personalization might be viewed as a threat to privacy. In research conducted by the Printing Industry Center at RIT, customers reported a preference for receiving U.S. postal mail from firms they already patronize.[9] Specifically, over three-quarters (82%) of the survey respondents liked getting catalogs from stores they frequent, and 67% also appreciated information about new products that they received from companies they patronize.

In this book, we will focus on printed customized marketing communications, including direct mail, catalogs, sales support materials created specifically for individual customers or dealers, and billing statements and other financial service information. The focus is on printed communications for two reasons. First, new technology in digital color printing allows for cost-effective, customized printed promotional material with nearly unlimited design possibilities. Second, print is the oldest form of communication mediated by technology—face-to-face interactions are older but are not mediated by technology.

How printing technology will fare in the emerging world of electronic media is of keen interest to those who follow the economic viability of U.S. industries. Printed communications in the U.S. still make up a significant part of the marketing communications budgets of most businesses. In a *DoubleClick* study of marketing executives in 2002, 86% reported that they use print advertising (e.g., magazine ads), 58% use direct mail, and 34% use catalogs.[10] The figures for domestic advertising expenditures in 2003 tracked by Universal McCann reveal that nearly $50 billion was spent on direct mail.[11] This represents 19% of the national spending on advertising media, up from $40 billion in 1998. While much of the attention on customized marketing communications has focused on the Internet as the fastest-growing direct advertising medium, printed communications continue to make up a large part of the marketing media expenditures in the U.S.

While direct mail is growing, unsolicited or unwanted direct postal mail, or *junk mail* as it is commonly called, is wasteful on both personal and environmental levels and depletes advertising budgets on the commercial level. Unsolicited mail currently represents about half of the mail U.S. households receive.[12] Some estimate that as much as half of the mail delivered to a single postal address does not get opened, but instead goes directly from the mailbox to the wastebasket.[13] While overall direct mail response rates increased slightly from 2.5% in 2003 to 2.7% in 2004,[14] specific industry sectors show much lower rates. For example, the over five billion credit card offers that were mailed in the U.S. in 2004 produced a response rate of less than 0.5%.[15]

Other challenges to the future of direct mail are concerns of privacy and data security. Consumers are increasingly voicing their choice to be removed from the mailing lists of firms they do not regularly patronize. As of May 2005, the Direct Marketing Association had 4,261,941 consumers on its Mail Preference Service.[16] Direct mail marketers are required to run their databases against this list and suppress the mail targeted to these individuals. As the number of "turned off" consumers grows, the long-term viability of the direct mail medium is in question. In addition, security breaches at financial services firms and information clearing houses such as ChoicePoint in 2005 have put nearly 50 million customers in the U.S. at risk.[17] If consumers refuse to share personal information with commercial firms because of security concerns, data-driven print will suffer from the loss of the information needed to make it work.

Unsolicited direct mail also poses an environmental problem. According to the EPA, 40% of America's trash is paper—71.6 million tons of it![18] The U.S. Postal Service estimates that in 2002 direct mail accounted for over two million tons of the volume of U.S. landfills.[19] While this is only a small proportion of the country's paper trash, direct mail is still vulnerable to criticisms from the environmental activists in the U.S.

The promise of this book is that the printing industry can eliminate both kinds of waste by creating relevant data-driven printed promotional materials using the latest database and digital printing technologies. Personally relevant marketing communications that are perceived as worthwhile by the receiver will reduce waste in both marketing budgets and environmental resources.

RATIONALE FOR THIS BOOK

Though the business case for customized marketing communications is strong, it requires the adoption of the latest digital color printing technology in order to implement sophisticated data-driven, content-rich, print campaigns. Based on our knowledge of the usually slow adoption patterns of any disruptive technology,[20] a research program was started in 2002 by the Printing Industry Center at RIT to ascertain the current status of customized print communications. We wanted to find out how customized print is being used, and why it is chosen instead of, or in addition to, other promotional options.

To set this in the media planning context, Chapter 2 describes the nature of integrated media planning and where data-driven print fits into the media mix. Then, Chapter 3 addresses the current scope of data-driven communication, the extent to which it is actually used, and barriers to its widespread adoption. We found two barriers to a more pervasive use of data-driven print: the lack of a top-level marketing strategy that benefits from a deep knowledge of customers, and the absence of the information technology infrastructure required to execute such a program. Chapter 4 addresses the marketing strategy barrier by introducing a new strategic framework that outlines the marketing goals of acquiring (A), serving (S), and keeping (K) customers where customized marketing communications make sense (creating the acronym *ASK*). Chapter 5 lays out the infrastructure requirements needed for successful implementation of these programs, including sections on database fundamentals (both for capturing customer information and organizing it for creating personalized messages), the software needed to create data-driven print communications, and the digital printing technology that produces the final printed pieces.

The latter part of the book addresses the print services provider and how he or she can create a business that fulfills the customized print needs of clients. The following two chapters detail how to build a data-driven print communications business. Chapter 6 identifies four successful business models for producing printed data-driven communications. One of these models is illustrated here at the end of the chapter in the case study of Standard Register's DesignOnDemand application to support Dealer Office Xpress (DOX), a common software program used in the automotive industry. Chapter 7 describes the organizational components needed for customized print communications, including human resources and sales strategies.

Chapter 8 covers measurement issues and how to design feedback systems to track communication effectiveness. To get the most out of any marketing program, reliable feedback must reveal whether the communication was received by the target audience and what its impact was. Feedback is key to determining financial gains and losses as measured by return on investment (ROI) or cost per response (CPR), two measures used historically by direct marketers. Chapter 9 summarizes the challenges of planning and implementing data-driven print, and provides a starting point for any business that wants to create a dialogue with its customers.

CASE STUDY 1.1: STANDARD REGISTER / DEALER OFFICE XPRESS (DOX)

In recent years, new variable data applications and the Internet have enabled a printer's customers to easily create targeted marketing campaigns. However, developing a system to facilitate this capability can be a major undertaking, especially for a printer without an extensive IT staff. To assist printers, companies are developing the necessary applications and then licensing their use to printers and their customers. This is commonly referred to as an application service provider (ASP) model. We recently had the opportunity to talk with Steve Couture of Standard Register's Print On Demand solution group to see how Standard Register is helping its customers more easily create personalized marketing communications over the Internet through its ASP system, DesignOnDemand® (DOD). Couture explained to us how Standard Register developed a customized DesignOnDemand application to support Dealer Office Xpress (DOX), a joint service of ADP and Standard Register, which serves the automotive and truck industry.

Currently there are more than 21,000 car dealerships in the U.S., most with information systems in place to manage their day-to-day business. Approximately 8,500 of these dealerships use ADP Dealer Management Systems (DMS). The capabilities of DMS mirror those of an enterprise resource planning (ERP) system, including modules to manage sales, vehicle financing, service, and accounting, as well as database marketing and campaign management.

Through the DOX program, Standard Register and ADP had become key suppliers of business forms to automotive and truck dealers. Some of these forms are used in conjunction with ADP's DMS system, but until the advent of DesignOnDemand, none of the documents were taking advantage of the vast quantity of information contained within the dealers' databases. Standard Register saw an opportunity for dealers to better leverage this information with DesignOnDemand. Powered by Standard Register's SMARTworks® technology, this powerful Web-based marketing tool was already being used in a variety of industries including insurance, managed care, and financial services to automate production of highly personalized marketing collateral.

Standard Register realized that integrating the DMS software with its DesignOnDemand application would enable dealerships to take advantage of their customer information to create customized customer communications. The new system would provide a true end-to-end fulfillment solution that could deliver full four-color communications and promotions within 48 hours of order placement.

In 2003, Standard Register approached ADP about developing a variable data printing solution for its DOX program, using customer relationship management (CRM) and other dealer management systems. The program's goals were:

1. to provide dealers with the ability to build lasting customer relationships by bringing customers back into the showroom and service departments,
2. to allow dealers to harness the power of their databases to specifically target individual customers or prospects,
3. to communicate special offers quickly and more efficiently, from thought-to-execution-to-print-to-distribution within 48 hours, and
4. to simplify marketing campaign development and execution with a system that dealers can use right at their desktops.

Released in January 2004, the customized DesignOnDemand application allows dealers to create 1-to-1 print communications "on the fly." During the development of the system, a key task was to create templates for personalized documents such as postcards, letters, brochures, and coupons, and to acquire digital assets such as logos and photographs of car models. The DOX DesignOnDemand application currently has 23 design templates for such products as jumbo postcards, small postcards, letters, and bi-fold self mailers, and gives dealers access to over 3,000 car photographs.

The DesignOnDemand product team decided to outsource the acquisition of the photographs that dealers would need. So, instead of incurring the expense of gathering photographs of all models of all new cars in all the available colors, Standard Register turned to AutoData, a company with a complete library of automobile images. A license agreement with AutoData makes it possible for dealerships to choose from any of the available pictures, and be charged only for what they use when they use it.

DesignOnDemand is useful to various dealership personnel, including parts and service managers, marketing managers, and sales managers. To get started, a dealership must have access to the DOX SMARTworks® Internet site. For this access, DOX charges a one-time installation fee and a monthly support fee for application maintenance. DesignOnDemand requires little training. It allows dealers to control their own messaging and branding, reducing advertising agency costs and the development, print, and distribution cycle time that agencies typically require.

Standard Register focused on automating as much of the process as possible through the back end of the system, enabling a dealership to create and order a mailing within 20 minutes. Dealers can query their own databases to find the exact population they want to target (e.g., those who need an oil change). Then they simply select the desired design template (a reminder postcard), customize it, and place the print order. A high resolution PDF file is transmitted to Standard Register and is automatically queued for printing (see Figure 1.1).

Another timesaving advantage of the system is that it eliminates the need for securing approval from senior management or corporate offices for every marketing piece because the design templates already integrate client-approved messaging and branding. Users can quickly create and send their mailings without delays.

Dealers can use the system to send customers sales promotions, new vehicle announcements, and service reminders for their vehicles. Although vehicle service accounts for only 11% of a dealership's revenue, this is actually represents 50% of its profit, so targeted mailings can provide dealers with an excellent return on their investment. DOD's targeted approach to marketing is attractive since car dealerships are facing increased competition from "quick lube shops" and small vehicle repair companies. Dealers can also alert customers when their leases are about to expire, and offer them incentives for signing new leasing agreements.

Once an order is submitted, it is routed to a Standard Register fulfillment center in Connecticut, California, North Carolina, or Texas. A variety of digital printing engines, including the Xerox 2060 and iGen3, and Kodak NexPress 2100 then print the materials. The prices for these applications are slightly higher than a typical mail-merge variable data application, but since most dealerships use higher levels of personalization anyway, the extra cost is justified by the ROI of the campaign.

Currently, DOX has 170 dealers using the new DOD software, and several hundred more are in line to install it. Standard Register has also customized DesignOnDemand to work with other dealer management providers, and more enhancements to the DOD system itself are on the horizon.

Figure 1.1 *DOX variable data mailing piece*

ENDNOTES TO CHAPTER 1

1. Neisser, *Cognitive Psychology.*
2. InfoTrends/CAP Ventures, *Production Workflow Solutions Product Compendium.*
3. Zahay and Griffin, "Information Antecedents of Personalization and Customization in Business-to-Business Service Markets."
4. Kotler, *Marketing Management.*
5. Gilmore and Pine, "The Four Faces of Mass Customization."
6. Godin, *Permission Marketing.*
7. Chakraborty, Lala, and Warren, "What do Customers Consider Important in B2B Websites?"
8. Manber, Patel, and Robison, "Experience with Personalization on Yahoo!"
9. Sorce, *Relationship Marketing Strategy.*
10. DoubleClick, *Spring 2002 Marketing Spending Index, http://banners.noticiasdot.com/termometro/boletines/docs/consultoras/doubleclick/2002/Doubleclick_estudio_2002_ingles.pdf.*
11. American Marketing Association, "2004 Marketing Fact Book."
12. U.S. Postal Service, *The Household Diary Study, http://www.usps.com/householddiary/welcome_print.htm.*
13. Wann, "Affluenza: Curing the Bug."
14. Direct Marketing Association, "The DMA 2004 Response Rate Study," *http://www.the-dma.org/research/.*
15. Campanelli, "Credit Card Solicitations at Highest in '04."
16. Direct Marketing Association, personal communication with the author, May 2005.
17. Dash, "Europe Zips Lips; U.S. Sells ZIPs," *http://www.ethics.org.au/ethics_forum/forum_posts.asp?TID=1142&PN=1.*
18. U.S. Environmental Protection Agency, "General Overview of What's In America's Trash," *http://www.epa.gov/epaoswer/non-hw/reduce/catbook/what.htm.*
19. U. S. Postal Service, "Lowering the Landfill Levels," *http://liteblue.usps.gov/news/link/2004june15_1.htm.*
20. Mahajan, Muller, and Wind, *New Product Diffusion Models.*

CHAPTER TWO

DATA-DRIVEN PRINT IN THE INTEGRATED MEDIA WORLD

THE PROBLEM: You are the manager for a local franchise hardware store, and have allocated $50,000 to spend on advertising. How should you spend it? On local newspaper ads? Cable television ads? Direct mail to households within five miles of your store? Radio ads? By purchasing billboard space? Or creating a promotional event involving hot air balloon rides in the parking lot? How does a marketing director choose one communications option over all the other ways it is possible to contact prospective and current customers?

Today more than ever there are a variety of media channels from which to choose when deciding how to reach an audience. In 2002 there were 280 national cable television networks, and this number is growing annually.[21] In 2004 the Oxbridge National Directory of Magazines counted 18,821 consumer magazines available in the U.S.[22] There are also millions of catalogs printed every year, and countless commercial Web sites. In this media-fragmented world, how do we choose among the alternatives?

The purpose of this chapter is to describe how media decisions are made for the purpose of implementing a marketing campaign. Marketing executives (who create marketing programs) often outsource media decisions to an advertising agency which in turn buys space or time in mass media outlets. Agencies may also work directly with a print services provider to produce printed materials such as direct mail and promotional brochures. In other cases, media decisions are made and implemented within the firm by the creator of the marketing strategy, usually the marketing manager or another senior executive. This executive may work directly with a print services provider or may produce the needed promotional materials with the firm's own internal resources. While this *insourcing* approach is often overlooked, it is an important alternative to consider. We will look at both methods of media decision-making.

THE MEDIA PLANNING PROCESS

Media selection is actually one of the last steps in planning the marketing strategy of a firm.[23] As shown in Figure 2.1, a media plan flows from the marketing goals of a firm. Let's say a consumer products firm wants to introduce an extension to its shampoo line. The new product will repair sun-damaged hair for active young women aged 18–34. The marketing plan will be made up of four elements (often referred to as the four Ps):

- development of the *product* itself,
- determining its *price* and the budget for the marketing campaign,
- creating the *promotion*al message, and
- "*placing*" that product for purchase by deciding what distribution channel(s) will be used.

All of these elements must be synchronized with the marketing strategy in order to create a successful plan. Two important elements of marketing strategy are the target market and marketing objective. In this example, let's say the product was developed to meet the needs of women who spend a lot of time in the sun and are worried about the effects of sun-damage to their hair. Let's say research has provided a demographic profile of this target audience: women 18–34 years of age who live in coastal states (e.g., Florida, California, and Texas).

Next comes the marketing objective that specifies a measurable outcome in order to determine whether the plan is successful. In this case, since the consumer products firm is extending an existing shampoo line, the marketing objective may be, for example, to increase shampoo sales by 3% by the end of the year in specific geographic areas (e.g., Florida, California and Texas). To do this, the marketers establish a standard price and an introductory promotional price (for example, $2.79 as the standard price with $0.50 off during a trial period). In order to create an incentive for retailers to stock and place the item on the shelf, channel promotions such as a retailer promotional allowance for an end-of-aisle display may also be budgeted.

Once the marketing objective and the target market are established, the next step is to devise an advertising plan. A compelling message must be created and delivered to the target market using some advertising medium or a combination of media, all to be paid for within a predetermined budget. Most consumer products firms use advertising agencies for these complex tasks. Agencies develop the creative elements, recommend the media, and implement the approved plan by producing the ads to be placed, and then buy space or time in the media selected.

The advertising planning process begins with specifying the promotional objective, which identifies the measurable response that is expected from the target audience after it has been exposed to the advertising. According to the standard hierarchy of effects,[24] most marketing communications planners realize that in order for a sale to result from advertising, consumers must:

- first, become aware of the product,
- next, be convinced that it will solve a problem they have,
- try it,
- and finally, perceive that it is the best option to solve the original problem, leading to a pattern of repeat purchasing.

In keeping with this approach, most promotional plans for new products identify awareness and trial as standard communications objectives. In the shampoo case, let's say the firm establishes the goal that 80% of the target audience would become aware of the product in six months' time. Once this objective is established, the message (content) of the advertising will be created. The choice of advertising media comes very late in the planning process, after the message has been determined and after the advertising budget has been allotted. Figure 2.1 summarizes this example.

Figure 2.1 *Sample marketing plan for new shampoo line extension*

PLAN ELEMENTS
I. Marketing objective: Improve shampoo sales by 3% by the end of the year in coastal states (e.g., Florida, California, Texas) II. Target market: women 18–34 years old who have sun-damaged hair III. Marketing mix (four Ps) a. Price: \$2.79 with \$0.50 off during trial period b. Product: line extension with extra conditioners built-in c. Distribution channel: place in current retail outlets d. Promotional plan: i. Objective: 80% of women aged 18–34 will be aware of the new product within six months ii. Channel promotion: allowance for end-of-aisle display iii. Advertising 1. Message: impact of harmful effects of sun exposure are offset by using the new product 2. Media options: television, magazines, radio, direct mail IV. Implementation V. Measuring results

With some exceptions, like IBM, many business-to-business (B2B) firms rarely use mass media to deliver advertising messages. B2B firms often have a smaller customer base (thousands rather than millions) and sell directly using their own sales force or regional value-added resellers, so the media choices for reaching their customers are less complex than for a consumer products firm. B2B marketing managers often create and implement promotional plans without the help of advertising agencies. However, a similar planning process is used. For these in-house marketing plans, the most frequently sought-after promotional objective is not awareness but lead-generation. A typical B2B marketing objective might be that 100 customers would inquire about the product or service within six months.

We have already seen that in the marketing planning process, selecting the actual media to be used is one of the last considerations the marketing manager or advertising agency will make. If a print services provider wants to get a piece of the marketing promotion budget, he or she must understand:

- who the decision makers are,
- what their role will be in the promotion planning process,
- the marketing objectives of the campaign, and
- how print will be able to deliver the firm's objectives of building awareness, generating leads, or getting an order in a cost-effective way.

The purpose of this chapter is to examine the media planning process from the perspective of the decision makers, whether they work for an advertising agency or are the marketing managers at a firm. In particular, we'll look at their perceptions about the effectiveness of print vs. broadcast media, and personalized vs. mass communication tactics.

THE ROLE OF THE ADVERTISING AGENCY IN MEDIA CHOICE

In the early 1900s, advertising agencies served as the sales agents for the only mass medium at the time—print. Agencies bought space in bulk from magazines and newspapers and then sold it to clients, adding a 15% commission as the primary source of revenue.[25] This system remained in place in the U.S. until the 1990s when, following the lead set by European agencies, one of the oldest agencies spun off its media buying unit. Today's media specialist buys space and time (for broadcast) from the major media outlets and sells them directly to clients or through agencies to their clients, all for much less than the traditional 15% surcharge.

But media planning and buying is still a major service of advertising agencies today. In a 2003 Printing Industry Center study,[26] advertising agencies were asked to name the top three services that they provide (see Table 2.1 and Appendix 2.1: Research Method Summary, p. 25). Media planning/buying was still the most common response, with nearly half of the agencies (48%) indicating it as a primary service. Creative development was the second most common response (43%), and customer relationship management was least common at 9%.

Table 2.1 *Primary services provided by advertising agencies*[27]

PRIMARY SERVICES OF AGENCY	PERCENT ANSWERED YES
MEDIA PLANNING/BUYING	48%
CREATIVE DEVELOPMENT	43%
GRAPHIC DESIGN	28%
SALES PROMOTION/COLLATERAL DEVELOPMENT	25%
PUBLIC RELATIONS	23%
BRAND CONSULTING	23%
DIRECT MARKETING	22%
DIGITAL BRANDING/WEB DEVELOPMENT	19%
CORPORATE IDENTITY	17%
OTHER SERVICES	12%
CUSTOMER RELATIONSHIP MANAGEMENT	9%

How does an advertising agency choose among the competing media? Traditionally, most advertising campaigns began with a large broadcast television media purchase,[28] but today multimedia and cross-media strategies are critical to successful business communications. Our research confirms the use of multiple outlets for clients. When the agencies in our study were asked to describe media allocations across their client base (see Table 2.2), broadcast media (television and radio) accounted for 18% of the agencies' media allocations, magazines were next at 17%, newspapers came in at 14%, collateral at 12%, and direct mail/direct marketing at 11%. "Other media" included Internet and outdoor advertising.

Though broadcast tops the list of media allocations in Table 2.2, print buying remains a mainstay of many agencies. Figure 2.2 gives an accounting of U.S. media expenditures in 2003, showing that ads in newspapers and magazines combined represented 23% of total expenditures, and

Table 2.2 *Media allocations for different media types across agency client base*[29]

MEDIA ALLOCATION CATEGORY	AVERAGE PERCENTAGE
BROADCAST (TV/RADIO)	18%
MAGAZINES	17%
NEWSPAPERS	14%
COLLATERAL	12%
DIRECT MAIL/DIRECT MARKETING	11%
STRATEGIC PLANNING	9%
OTHER PRINT MEDIA	9%
OTHER MEDIA	5%
MERCHANDIZING/POINT OF PURCHASE	4%
COMMERCIAL PHOTOGRAPHY	3%

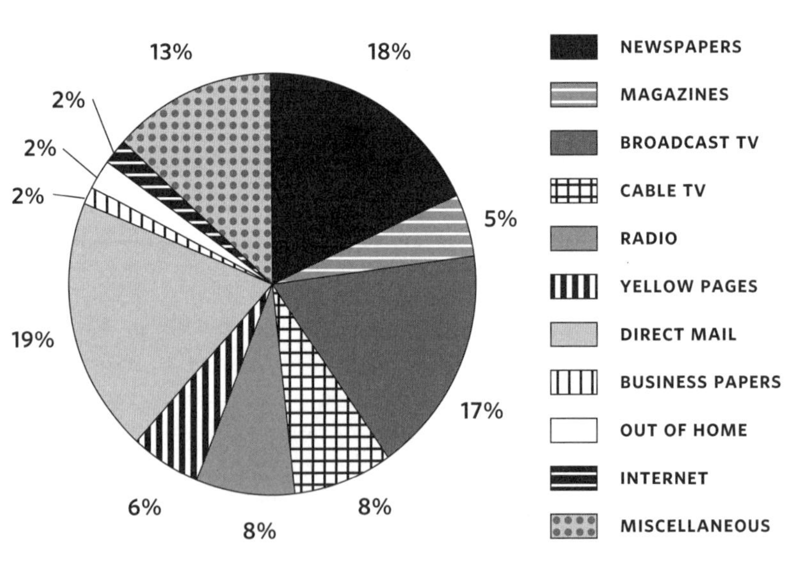

Figure 2.2 *2003 U.S. ad expenditures by media type*[30]

broadcast TV represented 17%.

As shown in Figure 2.2, advertising agencies don't limit their choices for what media to recommend to their clients to any one medium. Advertising agency respondents in the same Printing Industry Center study were also asked to indicate the top five factors that drive their media decisions for campaigns (Table 2.3). The top three responses were consistent with good media planning processes—select the medium that reaches the right target audience at the right price to deliver the marketing strategy.

Table 2.3 *Factors driving the media choices in a campaign*[31]

FACTORS*	PERCENT ANSWERING YES
TARGET MARKET SELECTION OR DEMOGRAPHIC	72%
COST/BUDGET	63%
MARKETING STRATEGY	56%
PAST HISTORY OF SUCCESS	43%
CLIENT SPECIFICATIONS	35%
ROI TARGET	31%
CREATIVE FLEXIBILITY	23%
NEED FOR MEASUREMENT	19%
TIME AVAILABLE	15%
AVAILABILITY OF DATA/DATABASES	15%
NEED FOR A NEW LOOK	15%
NEED FOR PERSONALIZED MESSAGES	14%

* *Respondents could indicate up to five factors.*

However, with the proliferation of media outlets and the problem of advertising clutter, advertisers are shifting away from major spending in broadcast media and leaning toward direct marketing.[32] This is likely a result of the increased accountability that clients are demanding from agencies. In a roundtable conversation with media planners, many observed that media planning is coming under more scrutiny to make the most of a client's marketing dollars.[33] As media executives in the roundtable forum noted, getting the most value out of advertising is their top concern. Direct marketing methods, in general, are well-positioned to deliver the accountability from marketing programs that clients are demanding in this economic climate. Whether it is a measure of lifetime value, return on investment, or cost per response, direct marketing has the advantage of a built-in measure of response. This need for accountability was mentioned by 31% of the agencies we surveyed, indicating that hitting an ROI target was an important consideration in campaign planning (see Table 2.3).

While the advertising agency can play a decisive role in selecting advertising media and executing ad campaigns, input from client firms is also critical. As shown in Table 2.3, client specifications are an important piece of the planning input (rated important by 35% of agencies). Understanding the client's media selection experience and preferences is crucial and will be detailed in the next section. This perspective is also important for those firms that do not use advertising agencies, because they must rely on their own knowledge of media or ask media consultants to help them.

THE ROLE OF THE MARKETING MANAGER IN MEDIA CHOICE

Another 2003 Printing Industry Center research study[34] of the marketing executives from manufacturing, financial services, and retail firms of varying sizes showed that 53% of the firms used the services of an advertising agency and almost half of them used two or more agencies (see Appendix 2.1: Research Method Summary, p. 25). Those with larger budgets utilized advertising agencies more frequently. This means that almost half of businesses, particularly smaller ones, rely on their own internal expertise to create and execute advertising plans. The purpose of this section is to understand the media allocation decision process of marketing managers, both those who use agencies and those who do not.

The marketing managers in the second study were asked how much they spent on a variety of media in the prior year, as shown in Table 2.4. The greatest proportion of the respondent firms' media budgets were spent on print advertising (35%), sales collateral (16%), Internet-based activities (5%), and direct mail (14%).

Table 2.4 *Media types and the percent of marketing managers' media budget spent on each*[35]

MEDIA TYPES	PERCENT OF BUDGET (MEAN)
PRINT ADVERTISING	35%
SALES COLLATERAL	16%
INTERNET-BASED ACTIVITIES	15%
DIRECT MAIL	15%
OTHER MEDIA	8%
EMAIL CAMPAIGNS	4%
RADIO ADVERTISING	4%
TELEVISION ADVERTISING	3%
OUTDOOR OR TRANSIT ADVERTISING	2%

The marketing budget of a typical firm was dispersed across several different media, with an average of 6.9% of corporate revenues dedicated to paying for these marketing communications.

Media choices are impacted by the target market.[36] Additional analyses revealed that financial services firms use more direct mail than manufacturing firms (21% versus 12%), because they often target their services directly to an individual consumer or household. On the other hand, manufacturing firms use more Internet-based advertising (19% versus 8%).

When buying print in particular, corporate marketing executives who do not use agencies can either buy print directly from print services providers or use the internal print capabilities that exist in many firms. Our results indicated that nearly two-thirds (64%) of the marketing executives who did not use advertising agencies bought printing directly from commercial printers. These commercial printers can provide different levels of service. For one-third of the respondents, commercial printers completely designed, produced, and distributed printed promotional materials. Other firms completed some of the work (such as the design) in-house, and then outsourced the print production to the commercial printer.

For firms with an in-plant print shop, 28% reported using in-house print resources wherever possible, outsourcing only particular print processes. But a dedicated print shop is not always necessary. Digital technology is growing the internal print capabilities of many firms. In our survey, over two-thirds of the respondents have the following print technologies: laser printers, black-and-white copiers, in-line ink jet printers, and digital color production devices. This allows them to produce relatively sophisticated, often personalized letters and other messages for their customers. Besides this direct advertising communication, 43% of respondents reported that they are increasing the amount of marketing collateral printed in-house due to the new design and printing technologies available to them.

As seen above, the creators of marketing strategies often have to implement those strategies as well, either through internal production resources or by contracting with specific media brokers. Because of the variety of media options open to a firm or an agency, the key question remains: If two media options can deliver a message to the same audience (e.g., direct mailing to households versus newspaper inserts), which one will the decision makers choose? Are there preferences that go beyond just the numbers?

MEDIA PERCEPTIONS

Because we also wanted to ascertain the media perceptions of advertising agencies and marketing executives, we asked both marketing executive and advertising survey respondents a series of broad-based statements about different media options. The respondents used a 5-point scale, which was later converted to generate the information in Table 2.5 below.

Table 2.5 *Media perceptions*[37]

STATEMENT	MARKETING EXECUTIVE*	ADVERTISING AGENCY*
Targeted campaigns outperform mass-market campaigns.	81%	67%
Broadcast media advertising is best for brand building.	40%	50%
When the company needs to know the direct ROI from a campaign, I use a direct-response medium.	33%	51%
Broadcast media advertising is best for driving store traffic.	27%	43%
We get better response rates with email campaigns than printed mail.	26%	19%

* *The percentage reported is for "agree" ratings of 4 or 5 combined.*

The majority of both the marketing executives and the advertising agencies expressed the perception that targeted campaigns outperform mass-market campaigns. This is consistent with the ideas of proponents of direct marketing, who preach the value of reaching the target audience with right-place, right-time, and right-message exactness.

What was surprising was the relatively low level of agreement with the statement that a direct response medium was the correct medium to use when return on investment (ROI) was important. Only one-third of the marketing executives and half of the advertising agencies agreed. Data-driven print will be selected over other media options only if printed direct response media are perceived as cost-effective. The delivery of a specific ROI for a campaign is the primary benefit of this medium. Clearly, there is a long way to go to convince marketers and their consulting agencies that this is true.

EFFICACY OF PRINTED MEDIA

Another issue we wanted to examine was how print is perceived by those making advertising decisions. Are print media in general viewed as viable in achieving marketing goals? Both marketing executives and advertising agency respondents were asked in what situations they would recommend print as a marketing communications tool.

While there was a similarity in the rank ordering of the top situations for both samples, a higher percentage of advertising agencies indicated that they "always" recommended print for most of the situations listed. As Table 2.6 shows, the introduction of a new product was the most common situation in which print was recommended as a marketing communications tool, with 77% of advertising agencies and 62% of marketing executives "always" recommending it. The second most common response was that print was especially useful for promotions or special offers at 75% and 49%, respectively. Increasing brand awareness followed at 74% and 38%, respectively. Cross-selling/up-selling was the least recommended situation for advertising agencies at 49%, and lead acquisition was the least-recommended situation for marketing executives, at 22%.

Table 2.6 *Recommending print as a marketing communications tool in specific situations*[38]

SITUATIONS RECOMMENDING PRINT	ADVERTISING AGENCY "ALWAYS"	MARKETING EXECUTIVE "ALWAYS"
INTRODUCE A NEW PRODUCT	77%	62%
PROMOTIONS OR SPECIAL OFFERS	75%	49%
INCREASE BRAND AWARENESS	74%	38%
BRAND POSITIONING	70%	33%
SALES SUPPORT	67%	24%
CUSTOMER RETENTION/LOYALTY	65%	33%
LEAD GENERATION	62%	22%
TO DRIVE RETAIL TRAFFIC	58%	24%
CUSTOMER ACQUISITION	57%	31%
CROSS-SELLING/UP-SELLING	49%	25%

The results indicate that while print is frequently recommended to serve a wide variety of functions, advertising agencies are more likely to recommend print to achieve a number of marketing goals than their marketing executive counterparts.

CONCLUSION

Both marketing executives and consulting advertising agencies can play an important role in the decision-making process for how marketing campaign budgets will be spent on various advertising media.

- Fifty-three percent of the manufacturing, financial services, and retail firms in our marketing executive study used the services of an advertising agency.
- Media planning/buying was the most common service that advertising agencies provided; nearly half of the agencies (48%) indicated this as a primary service. Creative development was the second most common service.
- Multiple media channels are often used in marketing campaigns. The factors that influenced media choice were consistent with good media planning processes—select the medium that reaches the right target audience at the right price to deliver the marketing strategy.
- When buying print in particular, many corporate marketing executives are the sole decision makers in the print buying decision. Nearly two-thirds (64%) of the marketing executives we surveyed used their internal corporate procurement function for this purpose.
- Print represents a substantial proportion of advertising spending and is seen as a versatile medium to achieve a variety of marketing objectives.

However, our research also gave us an indication of potential barriers that may be prohibiting the widespread use of data-driven direct marketing communications.

- Only one-third of the marketing executives and just half of the advertising agencies agreed (in Table 2.5) that "a direct response medium could be used when ROI was important."
- The need for personalization was mentioned (in Table 2.3) by only 14% of agencies surveyed as a top reason for selecting an advertising medium.

These are surprising statistics considering that "below the line" advertising (direct mail, marketing research, public relations, promotional events, and Internet marketing) is growing at twice the rate of traditional broadcast advertising, and the environment is right for the demand for data-driven print communication.[39] So, how much data-driven communication is out there? We'll investigate this in Chapter 3.

APPENDIX 2.1:
RESEARCH METHOD SUMMARY

A. The Advertising Agency's Role in Marketing Communications Demand Creation (PICRM-2003-05)

SAMPLE

The sample of 5,325 unique records was randomly selected from The Red Book list, which contains detailed profiles of nearly 13,500 U.S. and international advertising agencies. The agencies in the study were randomly selected by an automated phone dialing system. A total of 731 advertising agencies were contacted by phone to produce the 250 completed surveys for a completion rate of 34%. Of these 250 surveys, we established a quota of 100 completed questionnaires from direct-marketing agencies.

The advertising agencies that participated in the survey had an average of 56 employees, and their average annual billing was $26 million. Grouping the advertising agencies by billings revealed that 48% of those surveyed annually billed their customers for $5 million or less, another 39% billed from $5,000,001 to $50 million, and 13% reported over $50 million in annual billings.

The advertising agency respondents had worked an average of 19 years in the advertising industry and an average of 10 years for their current employers. Sixty-four percent of survey respondents had earned a college degree, and 20% had graduate degrees.

QUESTIONNAIRE

The choice of our specific questions was based on insights obtained through in-depth preliminary interviews with a number of advertising agencies about their interactions with clients, their media attitudes, and their experiences with personalized print. The final wording and order, and the percentage responding to each question, are presented in Appendix B of the original Printing Industry Center monograph, *The Advertising Agency's Role in Marketing Communication Demand Creation* (PICRM-2003-05).

PROCEDURE

A screener was used to identify the role of the interviewee within the advertising agency. The following titles qualified: media director, print production director, account executive, or creative director. Quotas were set for respondents who were classified as *strategy-focused* only (n=100) or *production-focused* (n=150).

B. Marketing Communications Demand Creation: Marketing Executive Study (PICRM-2003-06)

SAMPLE

The sample of 4,312 records was drawn from the Dun & Bradstreet list and was restricted to financial services firms, manufacturers, and retail firms. A total of 1,999 firms were contacted by phone to produce the 205 completed surveys. Of the completed surveys, 55 were from financial services firms, 100 were from manufacturing firms, and 21 were from retail establishments. Because we had difficulty filling the retail quota (we sought 50 retailers), we added 29 firms from a variety of other SIC codes. The list of SIC codes in the final sample are presented in Appendix A of the original Printing Industry Center monograph, *Marketing Communications Demand Creation: Marketing Executive Study* (PICRM-2003-06).

The final sample consisted of 67% male respondents. Nearly all of those surveyed had graduated from college or had graduate degrees. When asked about their roles in selecting media for their company's marketing campaigns, nearly 70% of the respondents said that they were part of a group of decision makers, and one quarter indicated that they were the sole decision makers regarding the selection of media.

Almost half of the respondents were from smaller firms (under 60 employees), and 26% were from larger firms (240 employees or more). Sixty-seven percent of the respondents characterized their firms as business-to-business (B2B) companies, and only 23% characterized their firms as business-to-consumer (B2C) companies.

The median size of the annual marketing communications budget was $300,000. The average size of the marketing communications budget was 6.9% of revenues (with a median of 2%). The respondents indicated that this figure did not include sales force compensation.

QUESTIONNAIRE

Insights into the specific questions to include were obtained by conducting in-depth interviews with a number of marketing executives about their interactions with advertising agencies, their media attitudes, and their experiences with personalized print. The final question wording and order, along with the percentage responding to each question, are presented in Appendix B of the original Printing Industry Center monograph, *Marketing Communications Demand Creation: Marketing Executive Study* (PICRM-2003-06).

21. National Cable & Telecommunications Association, *http://www.ncta.com/industry_overview/aboutIND.cfm?indOverviewID=58.*
22. American Society of Magazine Editors, "Number of Magazine Titles, 1988–2004," *http://www.magazine.org/Editorial/editorial_trends_and_magazine_handbook/1093.cfm.*
23. Kelley and Jugenheimer, *Advertising Media Planning.*
24. McGuire, "An Information Processing Approach to Advertising Effectiveness."
25. Cappo, *The Future of Advertising.*
26. Pellow, Sorce, Frey, Olson, Moore, and Kirpichenko, *The Advertising Agency's Role in Marketing Communication Demand Creation* (PICRM-2003-05).
27. Ibid.
28. Cappo, *The Future of Advertising.*
29. Pellow, et al., *The Advertising Agency's Role* (PICRM-2003-05).
30. American Marketing Association, *2004 Marketing Fact Book.*
31. Pellow, et al., *The Advertising Agency's Role* (PICRM-2003-05).
32. Schwartz, "Bigger and Bigger."
33. Anonymous, "Planning the Next Step."
34. Pellow, Sorce, Frey, and Banis, *Marketing Communications Demand Creation* (PICRM-2003-06).
35. Ibid.
36. Ibid.
37. Pellow, et al., *The Advertising Agency's Role* (PICRM-2003-05) and Pellow, et al., *Marketing Communications Demand Creation* (PICRM-2003-06).
38. Sorce and Pellow, *Demand for Customized Communications by Advertising Agencies and Marketing Executives* (PICRM-2003-08).
39. Schwartz, "Bigger and Bigger."

CHAPTER THREE

THE CURRENT STATE OF DATA-DRIVEN COMMUNICATIONS

IN CHAPTER 2 WE CONCLUDED THAT the current media planning environment could encourage the use of direct marketing campaigns because of its built-in capability to track response rates. However, our research showed that only one-third of media decision makers recommend such direct methods when they want return on investment (ROI) statistics for a campaign. In addition, less than 20% felt that the need for personalization was an important factor in campaign planning. These findings lead us to wonder how much customized marketing communication is actually being delivered in print, or in any other medium for that matter. This chapter examines this question.

Research conducted by RIT's Printing Industry Center benchmarked the amount and complexity of personalized advertising in the U.S.[40] Two distinct populations, advertising agencies and marketing executives, were queried because as we saw in Chapter 2, both play a role in media selection decisions. The marketing executive will often call on an advertising agency because of its history of media buying or at least its familiarity with media selection decisions in campaign execution. But almost half of the marketing executives we interviewed had not used an agency in the previous year, and many were able to print marketing materials in-house. Both groups were sampled to measure their current usage patterns and their underlying motivations for recommending personalization within the context of media planning and campaign execution.

AMOUNT AND COMPLEXITY OF PERSONALIZED COMMUNICATIONS

How many of today's marketing messages are personalized?[41] We can start by reviewing the data from various industry trade associations such as the Direct Marketing Association.[42] In its 2002 report on postal and email marketing, the DMA found that 62% of its members reported that they "sometimes" personalize information about a customer beyond name and address. A lower estimate emerged when print buyers were surveyed in a different study, with only 21% reporting that they bought variable data printing, a technology essential to producing personalized direct mail.[43] There is little convergence between these two estimates. The disparity may be explained by both the nature of the samples (existing heavy users vs. print buyers) and the questions asked (use of databases vs. specific production technologies).

Figure 3.1 illustrates the amount of personalization used annually by advertising agencies and marketing executives, based on the 2003 Printing Industry Center research monograph cited above.[44] An average of 23% (standard deviation = 27.11, median = 10%) of the work completed by advertising agencies involved personalization, and an average of 33% of the marketing executives' campaigns involved personalization (median = 25%). Only 3% of marketing executives had *not* produced a single personalized campaign in the previous year, and nearly 20% of the advertising agencies we surveyed had not produced a personalized campaign in the previous year.

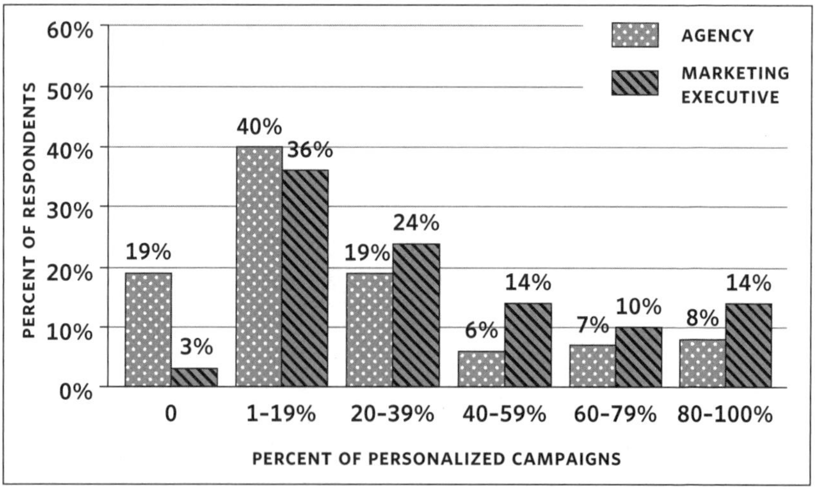

Figure 3.1 *Annual amount of personalization used*[45]

There are many ways that a campaign can be personalized and there are a variety of media to choose from. A personalized direct mail campaign can be produced simply by purchasing a list of prospective customers that fit a specific demographic or lifestyle profile and using traditional database marketing practices. In this case, the only data unique to the individual receiving the message will be his or her name, address, and salutation. More complex forms of customized marketing communications require specific data that capture the behavior of customers to produce unique messages that can vary their content in the text or graphics.

How much complexity in these personalized messages was normal? We asked our marketing executives and advertising agencies to distribute 100 points among five levels of complexity to indicate how often they used each level. The levels of personalized advertising complexity are defined in Table 3.1. Both of our respondent groups indicated that nearly half of their marketing campaigns used only the lowest level of complexity, the mail merge option, which includes only a variable address and/or salutation. Only 27% of the advertising agencies and 18% of the marketing executives used graphics in their customized messages.

Table 3.1 *Levels of complexity used in personalized campaigns*[46]

LEVEL	ADVERTISING AGENCY	MARKETING EXECUTIVE
Variable address and/or salutation	46%	50%
Variable address and/or numerical information in fixed fields	15%	19%
Variable address, text, and numerical information in dynamic fields	12%	14%
Variable text or numbers and graphics	14%	10%
Variable text or numbers and variable graphics	13%	8%

We were also curious whether these results would vary with the nature of the advertising agencies we contacted, and so we built our questionnaire to determine this as well. Advertising agencies that offered direct marketing as a primary service created the same percentage of personalized campaigns as those for whom direct marketing was not a primary service offering. There was also no significant difference in the complexity of the personalization produced by these two advertising agency groups. Correlations between advertising agency size and the amount or complexity of personalization were not significant either.

TYPES OF CLIENTS REQUESTING PERSONALIZATION

Advertising agency respondents who told us that their work involved some variable information or personalization were further asked to answer a series of questions about clients who typically requested personalization in their campaigns. Over three quarters of the clients (79%) who requested personalization were categorized as small clients, with annual revenues of $100 million or less. Another 15% of clients requesting personalization were classified as medium-sized, with annual revenues of $101 million to $1 billion. Only 6% were large clients, with annual revenues of over $1 billion.

Nearly half of the clients (47%) who requested personalization were B2B companies, and another 42% were primarily B2C companies. The remaining 11% were categorized as both.

The two client industry classifications that most often requested personalization were manufacturing and retail, both at 40%. The financial industry requested personalization 34% of the time, and the pharmaceutical industry requested personalization 16% of the time.

FACTORS IMPACTING THE LEVEL OF PERSONALIZATION

Awareness

Innovations in digital color printing technology in the last decade have greatly expanded the creative options for data-driven direct postal mail. Though the first digital color presses were slow and somewhat unreliable, the latest models can produce high-quality color graphics at a cost only slightly higher than conventional offset printing for short runs.[47] Consistent with the technology adoption model, a company must first be aware of new technology before it can try or adopt it.[48]

Do advertising agencies realize what the new printing technology can do? Are marketing executives aware of the digital color printing innovations that can enable their printed communications to be personalized? While full service advertising agencies often serve as the principal suppliers for mass media communications, much direct response material is handled in-house.[49] A study conducted on behalf of the Printing Industries of America (PIA) indicates that media planners are more involved in the selection of "measured" media—those monitored by services that measure advertising expenditures—than they are in direct mail or sales collateral.[50]

As shown in Table 3.2, nearly two thirds of our research study groups were aware of the new printing technologies used for personalization. However, while over half of the advertising agencies had shown samples to their corporate clients, only 36% of the marketing executives reported that they had been shown samples by their agencies. The marketing executives' lower levels of exposure to printing samples of new technology may be explained in part by the percentage that had been using an advertising agency the year before the study was conducted. (We had found that only 53% of the marketing executives in our sample had used an advertising agency in the year prior to the study.)

Table 3.2 *Awareness of personalization print technologies*[51]

AWARENESS STATEMENT	ADVERTISING AGENCIES*	MARKETING EXECUTIVES*
I am aware of new print technology for personalization.	64%	62%
I have (been) shown samples of printed communications using these new technologies.	57%	36%

**The respondents used a 5-point scale, where "5" means "strongly agree." The percentage reported is for "agree" ratings of 4 or 5 combined.*

Strategic Need

What accounts for the relatively modest use of complex personalization? A clue can be found in the factors that had an impact on the media decisions of our ad agency respondents. Target market selection was the most important factor, followed by cost, budget, and marketing strategy. Personalization was not a major consideration in media selection, and in fact was rated as important by only 13%. In addition, 43% of the ad agency respondents indicated that past history with specific media types was an important consideration in media planning. While new media options are considered, advertising agency executives still have a strong tendency to revert to familiar alternatives. Advertising agencies may only recommend complicated data-driven campaigns if they have had previous success with this technology.

NECESSARY CONDITIONS FOR THE ABILITY TO USE DATA-DRIVEN PRINT

The advertising agencies that reported that less than 10% of their work involved variable information or personalization were asked why they did not use more of it. The most common obstacle keeping these respondents from recommending personalization strategies to their clients was price, at 28%, with lack of a suitable database following at 23%. Nearly half of the respondents stated that "some other obstacle" kept them from recommending personalization to their clients. Of this last group, nearly one-third wrote in that there was a lack of need for this type of advertising strategy.

The marketing executive respondents that reported using a lower level of personalization were also asked about obstacles. Lack of resources (money, databases, people, or knowledge) and lack of need were the top obstacles mentioned.

Because we realized that a solid information infrastructure was critical to implementing a personalized communications program, we also elicited responses about the basic requirements for executing different levels of complexity in personalization.

The marketing executives were asked to indicate whether they maintained a database of their customers internally or through an outsourced third party. The majority of the respondents (94%) indicated that they maintained the database internally. Only 21% reported that they used a customer relationship management (CRM) system. The software they used for their CRM and customer database systems varied widely—over 160 software packages were mentioned. When the marketing executives were asked which capabilities they used in managing their customer databases, nearly 60% said they used sales force management, 31% used data mining, and 28% used campaign management.

We were curious to see whether those firms with more data management and analysis resources also used more complex forms of personalized messages in their marketing communications programs. Additional analyses were conducted[52] on the results to determine whether firms that had CRM systems and used data mining and campaign management software used more complex forms of personalization. Table 3.3 presents the means for the use of CRM, data mining, and campaign management tools in terms of the percent of campaigns that used personalization and the complexity of the personalization.

The amount of personalized campaigns did not vary in relation to any of the database technology applications. That is, whether firms had a CRM system or not, or did or did not use data mining or campaign management, the average amount of campaigns that were personalized still ranged from 32% to 35%. However, the complexity of the personalization was impacted by the data resources of the firm. Specifically, the second level complexity, where variable address and/or numerical information are placed into fixed fields, was used more by those firms who had CRM systems than by those that did not, 27.6% and 15.1% ($p = 0.01$) respectively. This level was also used more by those possessing data mining capabilities (25.8%) than those that did not (14.7%, $p = 0.01$). The middle level of complexity, where variable address, text, and/or numerical information are placed into dynamic fields, was used more frequently by those with campaign management tools (22.1%) than those without (10.5%, $p = 0.01$). There were no differences in the use of the two highest levels of complexity in relation to the presence of database technology systems in the firm.

Table 3.3 *Database functions and level of personalization used*[53]

	USE OF CRM		USE OF DATA MINING		USE OF CAMPAIGN MANAGEMENT TOOLS	
	YES	NO	YES	NO	YES	NO
Percent of campaigns personalized	35.2%	34.9%	32.2%	34.4%	32.3%	34.2%
LEVEL OF COMPLEXITY						
Variable address and/or salutation	45.3%	50.3%	46.5%	50.8%	44.7%	51.3%
Variable address and/or numerical information in *fixed* fields	27.6*	15.1*	25.8*	14.7*	20.0	18.4
Variable address, text, and numerical information in *dynamic* fields	16.1	12.9	12.9	15.2	22.1*	10.5*
Variable text or numbers and *graphics*	9.2	11.8	9.7	10.9	8.6	11.2
Variable text or numbers and *variable graphics*	4.2	9.9	6.8	8.2	6.3	8.4
N	33	79	48	78	41	85

* *Significant at p < .01, ANOVA*

We conducted another test to determine whether the frequent use of personalization was related to more complex forms of personalization. A correlation analysis was performed to test the number of personalized campaigns implemented and the complexity level of the personalization. As shown in Table 3.4, those firms that conducted more personalized campaigns reported a more frequent use of the highest level of customization ($r = .214$, $p < .05$).

Table 3.4 also presents the correlation between firm demographics (the size of firm and percent of media budget spent on direct mail) and the amount and degree of personalization used. There were two significant correlations discovered. More personalized campaigns were used by smaller firms ($r = -.181$, $p < .05$) and those with a larger percentage of their media budget spent on direct mail ($r = .207$, $p < .05$).

Table 3.4 *Correlations with level of complexity*[54]

	PERCENT OF CAMPAIGNS PERSONALIZED	SIZE OF FIRM	PERCENT OF MEDIA BUDGET SPENT ON DIRECT MAIL
Percent of campaigns personalized		−.181*	.207*
LEVEL OF COMPLEXITY			
Variable address and/or salutation	−.150	.048	.009
Variable address and/or numerical information in *fixed* fields	−.053	−.085	−.003
Variable address, text, and numerical information in *dynamic* fields	.064	.131	.153
Variable text or numbers and *graphics*	.095	.026	−.112
Variable text or numbers and *variable graphics*	.214*	.041	−.146
N	148	111	163

* *Significant at $p < .05$*

We also tested whether the nature of the database applications varied by industry. Financial services firms used significantly more data mining (48%) and campaign management tools (46%) than other types of firms. When broken down by firm size, larger firms were more likely to use data mining (39%) than smaller firms (21%). Firms with larger advertising budgets ($1 million and over) used data mining, campaign management, and data cleansing software significantly more than those with smaller budgets. However, there were no differences by size of marketing budget or industry in whether a firm had a CRM system.

CONCLUSIONS

There is significant discussion in marketing circles about customized marketing communications and 1-to-1 marketing. Consultants tout the value of reaching the target audience with right-place and right-time exactness. One-to-one marketing, they claim, allows firms to use knowledge about customers' preferences to rise above the din of competitive messages. Based on our survey results, though, neither the advertising agencies nor their corporate clients have broadly embraced campaigns designed around these principles. Sixty-four percent of the advertising agency respondents agreed that they were aware of the technology and 57% reported that they had shown samples of these campaigns to clients, but only 23% of the work they created used variable data. Moreover, 46% of the advertising agencies' variable-data jobs and half of the marketing executives' jobs involved only a simple mail merge. Personalization has value only if the individual views it as relevant. A mail merge does not create relevance. Consumers need offers that are directed to them and their specific needs.

Those firms that conducted more campaigns had more information resources (CRM, data mining, and campaign management systems). In addition, the firms with more information resources used more complex forms of personalization. More personalized campaigns were used by smaller firms and those with a history of using direct methods.

In this context, the results from this research would indicate that the glass is "half-full." That is, nearly three-quarters of the sample had used personalized methods in the past, but only about half of the time did they use personalized elements in the message that went beyond name, address, and salutation. What accounts for the current low use of complex customization? Perhaps it is still too new. When we asked our advertising agencies (in Chapter 2) to indicate the top five factors that affect the media decisions for their campaigns, they chose target market selection as the most important factor, followed by cost, budget, and marketing strategy. Personalization was not a major consideration in media selection, since it was rated as important by only 13% of the ad agency respondents. However, 43% indicated that past history with specific media types was an important consideration in media planning.

Advertising agency executives still have a strong tendency to revert to familiar alternatives, and may only recommend complicated customized campaigns if they have had previous success with this technology. This might explain why although nearly two thirds of the advertising agency respondents were aware of the new personalized print technologies, only slightly more than half had shown samples to clients (presumably recommending them as options).

Still, simple personalized campaigns may play a useful role for smaller firms or those new to direct marketing activities. A laddering strategy could be used to recommend personalization to new clients of direct marketing. First, a firm could start with a simple personalized campaign to demonstrate the effectiveness of direct methods. Even if its existing database infrastructure is weak, success using a good list can be achieved through outsourcing. As the firm's knowledge of its customers grows and its database infrastructure capabilities mature, the firm will be able to confidently use more complex forms of personalization. It is likely that this approach is being used by practitioners today given the long sell cycle in direct marketing business development.

Since personalization offers such benefits as improved response rates and increased return on marketing investments, we asked some of our advertising agency people why they did not recommend it more frequently. The biggest obstacles were price, lack of a suitable database, and the client's lack of perceived need. In face-to-face interviews it became apparent that the price factor was linked to the expense associated with building the appropriate data infrastructure for successful execution of a customized campaign. The reluctance to recommend an untested technology, coupled with the challenges of acquiring and maintaining a database of customer information beyond name and address, are important barriers to overcome. The last barrier, lack of perceived need, shows that the starting point is to identify the ways data-driven print communication can be used to deliver improved marketing results.

The next two chapters outline various ways to overcome these barriers. Chapter 4 identifies a strategic framework for data-driven print, and Chapter 5 describes the information technology infrastructure itself, and what digital print technologies are needed to make the best use of it.

ENDNOTES TO CHAPTER 3

40. Sorce and Pellow, *Demand for Customized Communications by Advertising Agencies and Marketing Executives* (PICRM-2003-08).
41. The terms "personalized" and "personalization" are used throughout this chapter because the research presented here used this term rather than *customized marketing communication* or *data-driven print*.
42. Direct Marketing Association, *The State of Postal and E-Mail Marketing*.
43. WhatTheyThink.com, *Print Buyers Survey on Variable Data Printing*.
44. Sorce and Pellow, *Demand for Customized Communications* (PICRM-2003-08).
45. Ibid.
46. Ibid.
47. Riggs, "Printing and Production: A Tight Fit," *http://directmag.com/mag/marketing_printing_production_tight/index.html.*

48. Rodgers and Chen, "Post-Adoption Attitudes to Advertising on the Internet."
49. McArthur and Griffin, "A Marketing Management View of Integrated Marketing Communications."
50. Graphic Arts Marketing Information Service (GAMIS), *Media Planning and Print Selection*.
51. Sorce and Pellow, *Demand for Customized Communications* (PICRM-2003-08).
52. Sorce and Pellow, "Amount and Complexity of Personalization in Marketing Campaigns."
53. Ibid.
54. Ibid.

CHAPTER FOUR

A STRATEGIC FRAMEWORK FOR DATA-DRIVEN PRINT

WE HAVE SEEN THAT customized marketing communications do not stand alone. It takes a comprehensive marketing program to achieve a business objective. Whether you are an advertising agency executive advising a client, a marketing manager planning a campaign, or a print services provider trying to sell data-driven print, understanding the corporate strategy of your internal or external client is the necessary starting point.

Marketing strategies flow from and are consistent with the broader corporate strategy.[55] The marketing strategy determines which target markets will receive certain products and services. According to Treacy and Wiersema, there are only three basic *value disciplines* of successful marketing strategies:

- product leadership, built on superior product or service innovation,
- operational excellence, built on superior internal operations, and
- customer intimacy, built on superior customer service and knowledge.[56]

These value disciplines will be crucial in formulating a *value proposition*, the set of benefits the firm offers to its customers to satisfy their needs.[57] The value proposition will determine the product positioning and subsequent copy used in advertising and other promotions. Firms that select a product leadership strategy will need to identify for the consumer the benefits of superior quality. For example, one well-known tire company translates its superior quality into the benefit of safety and peace of mind for the consumer. Firms that select an operational excellence strategy may create advertising that stresses the benefit of reliability by guaranteeing that the order will arrive when promised. Firms using the customer intimacy strategy may create a value proposition of customer convenience by showing that customers can use the firm's databases to keep track of their own purchase history so that, for example, in case of a warranty service need, the customer will not need to produce the original dated sales receipt.

All marketing messages, whether they are delivered via mass media advertising, sales promotion material, the firm's Web site, or direct marketing, should reinforce the strategic value discipline selected by the firm. Data-driven communications must be integrated into the wide-ranging initiatives designed to achieve the marketing goals of the firm. Ultimately, there are three basic marketing objectives to achieve revenue growth. We will coin the acronym *ASK* as a short-hand for these objectives.

MARKETING STRATEGY AND OBJECTIVES: JUST *ASK* (ACQUIRE, SERVE, KEEP)

This chapter defines the marketing strategy context for implementing a data-driven communication program. As we explore the print options for customized marketing communications, we will describe the purpose of the program in terms of meeting three specific marketing objectives:

- **A**cquire new customers,
- **S**erve existing customers well, and
- **K**eep the profitable customers and prune the unprofitable ones. ***ASK!***

In more formal language, firms can build their businesses through:

1. demand generation—building awareness, inducing trial or inquiry, and motivating the first purchase;
2. insuring customer satisfaction via transaction and fulfillment—generating orders, providing a service, fulfilling orders, or, as in the case of printed statements, providing records of buyer/seller transactions; and
3. building the long-term value of customers—increasing retention and loyalty, resulting in a larger share of wallet, or share of mind, from existing customers.

The acronym *ASK* reinforces the basic direct marketing principle that in all cases, whether the marketing communications are created to acquire, serve, or keep customers, an organization must first *ask* customers for permission to use information about their identities, needs, and interests for future marketing efforts.

This chapter provides an overview of how customized marketing communications can achieve each of these three objectives. At its conclusion, specific tactics will be described as alternative approaches for implementing a print-centric, data-driven, marketing communication program.

ACQUIRING NEW CUSTOMERS

Although the term is new, "data-driven print" describes what direct marketing professionals have been doing for years to help businesses build their customer bases by acquiring new customers. A survey conducted by the DMA in 2002 indicated that direct postal mail or email is used most often for customer and order acquisition.[58] Specifically, 46% of postal mail and 31% of email is designed to generate orders, and 27% of both postal mail and email is designed to generate leads. This contrasts with 11% of postal mail and 18% of email that is used for building customer loyalty or improving customer retention.

How can data-driven communications bring in new customers? Frequent users of direct mail revealed that their mailing strategies include customizing mailings according to a profile (76% "sometimes" use this strategy), mailing to certain geo-demographic segments (67%), and creating new targets through an analysis of prospect files (42%).[59] These prospect files are compiled by list vendors that group people or businesses based on specific demographic, lifestyle, or purchasing data. Firms frequently send undifferentiated and often unsolicited mail to customers that have been selected based on their predicted interest in a product as a result of past purchase behavior or some correlated demographic descriptor.

Direct mail that varies only by the receiver's name and address is the simplest form of data-driven communication. This junk mail, or "spam," in the case of email, is rarely perceived as valuable. In fact, many adults register on do-not-mail lists and buy spam-blocking software to avoid it. Consistent with this negative perception, the response rates to these communications are very low. When only a small amount of information is known about each prospective customer, the offer, message, or promotion is not usually highly relevant to those who receive it. For example, women's apparel catalogs may be mailed to lists of women who have purchased apparel through direct mail catalogs. These catalogs may miss the mark completely for a woman who has only bought children's clothing for a grandchild and not has purchased any apparel for herself. The demographic of gender is also not a good predictor of a specific need for a product. This is why prospecting efforts based on demographic profiles alone often yield low response rates. Customization works best when it is relevant.

In order to make customization relevant, firms need specific information about individual prospects. In order to elicit information from potential customers, consumer products companies often start with mass media to distribute messages to a broadly-defined target market. This mass audience allows a B2C firm to cast a broad net to reach those yet unidentified customers who "need" its product or service. Interested customers are identified when they reply by dialing an 800 number, sending back a reply card, or visiting a Web site. B2B firms may collect business cards from visitors to a trade show exhibit. In either case, the potential customers, or *hand-raisers*, as they are called, request information from the seller.

An example of this approach was described in a recent article in the *Inside 1-to-1* e-newsletter published by the Peppers and Rogers Group.[60] Late in 2004, business trade magazines carried an advertising campaign by Jaguar announcing the new XJ8L model. The print ads included a tear-out card asking interested customers to share information about themselves. Along with the traditional name and address, Jaguar also asked potential customers to identify at what stage in the purchase process they were, and what factors they considered important in determining the next car model they would buy. The campaign produced an immediate 40% jump in lead generation, and allowed Jaguar to understand its customers better. Jaguar advertising professionals went to great lengths in the wording of the card to capture the specific needs of each customer. For example, if a prospect only wanted to be mailed a brochure, a street address was requested but not an email address. In Jaguar's plan, mass media was initially used to find likely prospects, and it is likely that customized marketing communications will be sent next to move the hand-raisers along their various paths toward purchasing a vehicle.

For firms that work through dealers or other value-added resellers, marketing communications can be customized to serve the various locales of the geographically-dispersed resellers. For example, at a local car dealership, the customization of a brochure could reflect local conditions (e.g., the season or time of year, local landmarks appearing in photographs, or offers that reference other local dealers or a specific customer base) and at the same time maintain a nationally consistent corporate look and feel, which is important to national branding efforts. A manufacturer could also help dealers communicate with their customers through co-op advertising in local newspapers or on television, point-of-sale displays or posters, or zip-targeted mailings. With the correct infrastructure in place, a dealer could use Internet-distributed corporate display templates that would allow space for him or her to customize content as needed, and receive the resulting full-color, large-format posters within 24 hours of submission from a local print provider who has a contract with the corporate office. These posters in dealers' windows are designed to draw in the casual shopper to take advantage of special price promotions.

As reported in *Investing in Digital Color... The Bottom Line,*[61] one such dealer-driven customized campaign was developed by Lexinet for Coldwell Banker. The objective of the program was to generate additional real estate listings in neighborhoods served by their agents. A postcard was sent to neighbors after the listing of a home (see Figure 4.1). Local agents did not have the expertise to design, print, and find mailing lists of households in their regions, but relied on Lexinet to design a template where text and pictures specific to one agent's listing could be uploaded via the Internet to create a customized postcard mailing. Lexinet managed the printing process and mailing. Sometimes the agents used their own lists of residents, but in many cases Lexinet provided mailing lists selected by zip code. The postcard could be customized by each agent with contact information and a photograph. The goal of the campaign was to build awareness of real estate agents within specific geographic areas, so when homeowners were ready to sell, they would remember these agents and call on them. In a way, the postcard became a pseudo-personal recommendation by a neighbor: "Use this agent, as we are doing, and sell your home fast and for what it's worth." Though the agent only knew the names and addresses of those who received the mailing, the information was nevertheless highly relevant to them because it referred to their own neighborhoods.

Figure 4.1 *Coldwell Banker customized direct mail postcard*

In sum, communications consultants trying to help a firm start a customized marketing communications program should recommend that the client begin by using an information acquisition strategy. A direct response reply request delivered by mass media is a relatively low risk approach. Over time, as the client builds a customer database, he or she can leverage this information for more sophisticated customization efforts.

SERVING CUSTOMERS BY FULFILLING THE PROMISE

Once a customer has indicated an interest in a new product or service or has made an initial trial purchase, the firm must now deliver on its promised offer. The focus on customer service was a hallmark of the quality era of management thinking that grew in popularity in the 1980s and still persists today in the guise of six-sigma programs.[62] For some product categories, this is the primary way to build *customer equity*. See the discussion of Customer Equity below.

CUSTOMER EQUITY

In the book *Driving Customer Equity*,[63] the newly defined construct of *customer equity* describes three ways to build value for a customer:

1. *Value equity* is a customer's objective assessment of the utility of a brand. This assessment is driven by the product's quality, price, and convenience.
2. *Brand equity* is a customer's subjective and intangible assessment of the brand, built through image and meaning. This assessment is influenced by brand awareness, consumer attitudes toward the brand, and the firm's corporate citizenship.
3. *Retention equity* is the tendency of a customer to "stick with" a brand above and beyond objective and subjective assessments. This tendency is fostered by loyalty programs, special recognition and treatment, community building, and marketing communication built on predictive models of customer preferences.

To some extent, the nature of a product will determine which type of customer equity is the right one for a firm to pursue. But in most cases, all three types of equity will be part of the equation in any marketing program, though the balance will shift among different product categories. Finding the right equity balance is the challenge for all marketing managers.

Customers will often mention a history of successful transactions when describing the characteristics of businesses they like to patronize.[64] Transactional exchange involves the transfer of something tangible or intangible between parties.[65] If the consumer's goals are fulfilled by the product or service, this leads to a sense of pleasure and satisfaction that increases the likelihood that the consumer will buy again.

Transactional marketing strategies are still important even now that customer relationship management (CRM) has become common (more on CRM in the next section). Coviello, Brodie, Danaher, and Johnston measured the frequency with which transactional versus relational exchange strategies are used in business practice, and found that about one-third of firms still use a transactional marketing strategy.[66] These firms are likely to be large B2C consumer products firms. Firms that tend towards relationship strategies are often B2B service firms, where face-to-face interactions stimulate the growth of commitment, trust, and cooperation between buyer and seller. This is consistent with O'Malley and Tynan's hypothesis that the opportunity to develop relationships is "only feasible for high-involvement products characterized by inelastic demand where regular interaction with consumers occurs."[67] For example, the vintage instrument enthusiast who will pay just about any price for a rare guitar would be a better candidate for relationship marketing than the parent who is shopping for an instrument for a child's possibly fleeting interest in playing a musical instrument.

Service is the starting point for building a connection with customers. Responsiveness and accuracy of customer-generated information allows for superior customer service. For large firms that have multiple outlets and customer "touch points," information technology is used to create a single view of the customer, enterprise-wide.[68] These systems allow the customer to efficiently access transaction history information, the status of an order, or the amount of money left on a credit line either directly through a Web site, or by phone or face-to-face interactions with company representatives.

How do printed data-driven communications support a transaction marketing strategy for fulfillment? For many consumers, the printed record of the buying exchange is viewed as an important part of the transaction. These records may be utility billing statements, monthly financial balance statements, or annual health care insurance contracts. Though e-billing is growing, a majority of customers still want accurate and up-to-date printed records of their transactions. One quarter of all first-class mail is from financial services companies and a large percentage of that is transaction-based.[69]

Once seen as a simple record of transactions, monthly statements can also deliver information about additional services for sale. For example, a telecommunications firm can detect how many local toll calls an individual customer makes, and may suggest that the customer switch to a new plan that features free local calls. (But the monthly basic service fee may be higher. Read the fine print!) Monitoring the balances of its customers allows a bank to suggest additional financial products or services that fit the financial status of each customer. For firms with a frequent buyer program, customized communications based on an individual's transactions will trigger offers that shoppers may find hard to resist.

For all of these scenarios to work, the selling firm needs information about the customer and the ability to leverage it. A leader in strategic thinking around billing and statement communications is DST Output. Using sophisticated databases of information about their clients' customers, DST Output creates customized offers that include value-added information on standard transaction reports. A profile of DST Output is found in the case study at the end of the chapter.

Data-driven print communications are an essential element of transactional exchanges for many types of businesses since the printed record of the transaction is viewed as part of the product. The promotional implications of these databases are just now being explored and offer a wealth of information for a firm to use in cross-selling and up-selling services.

KEEPING PROFITABLE CUSTOMERS AND BUILDING LIFETIME VALUE

Fueled by the rhetoric of the 1-to-1 gurus, many marketers have been encouraged to build relationships with their current customers in order to improve profitability. Given the high cost of acquisition, more profit can usually be extracted by increasing customer retention rates (often used as a surrogate indicator of loyalty). Though some have questioned the link between profitability and loyalty,[70] others have described improved profits as a result of building loyalty through relationship marketing.[71]

When designing a relationship marketing program, it is helpful to understand the history of relationship marketing and the theories that describe the dynamics between buyers and sellers. The notion of relationship marketing migrated to the business and marketing psychology fields from organizational behavior and industrial marketing research, where interdependence between firms has been identified as the foundation of successful B2B alliances. Morgan and Hunt defined relationship marketing in 1994 as all marketing activities directed towards establishing, developing, and maintaining successful relational exchanges.[72] In defining this key construct, Morgan and

Hunt drew from social and clinical psychology, namely, the social exchange theory and the marriage literature. In their model, commitment and trust were key mediating variables because they encourage exchange partners to preserve relationship investments, resist attractive short-term alternatives, and maintain the belief that partners will not act opportunistically.

In the B2B world, the relationship between firms is usually developed through face-to-face interactions over a long time period, fostering a sense of mutual interdependence.[73] However, there has been a healthy debate among researchers about whether relationship marketing strategy is appropriate for explaining B2C exchanges. Sheth and Parvatiyar claim that the application of relationship marketing to the consumer is logical: "When producers and consumers directly deal with each other, there is a greater potential for emotional bonding that transcends economic exchange. They can understand and appreciate each others' needs and constraints better, are more inclined to cooperate with one another, and thus, become more relationship oriented."[74] Consumers' willingness to engage in relationships with businesses, they argue, is evidenced by their participation in loyalty programs. However, Sorce and Edwards have found that customers rarely described participation in a loyalty or frequent buyer program in their definitions of what a relationship with a commercial firm meant to them.[75] Furthermore, Pressey and Mathews found that relationship marketing concepts were associated with the patronage of personal service establishments such as hairdressers and recreation centers, where face-to-face interactions were the norm.[76]

If you don't match the right strategy to the right customers, a relationship marketing program will fail. And there are plenty of examples of CRM gone awry. As noted by Fournier, Dobscha, and Mick, "The very things that marketers are doing to build relationships with customers are often the things that are destroying them."[77] For example, when firms want to reward frequent buyers, they provide special services to "prestige" customers. Other customers who are loyal but don't buy as frequently as the "prestige" customers might not qualify as quickly to receive the special deals. These other customers want their loyalty to be rewarded too, and may resent the fact that they aren't getting special treatment.

So, how does a firm avoid these pitfalls and benefit from a relationship marketing strategy? A successful example is found in the entertainment industry. A 2003 article in the *Harvard Business Review* reported on the success of database marketing for Harrah's casinos.[78] Harrah's transformed the frequent user program it developed in 1997, "Total Gold," to one that was more personalized. Total Gold had been designed to provide regular customers with incentives to visit Harrah's casinos throughout the country. Slot machine players inserted their Total Gold cards into the machines and earned credits as they played, which rewarded them with free hotel rooms, dinners, show tickets, and gift certificates. The program was very similar to what other casinos were offering, however, and so did not build customer loyalty. As will happen with any undifferentiated program, the customers simply took their free benefits (in this case, rooms and dinners) and then moved on (in this case, to other casinos for more gambling). One benefit of Total Gold was that it provided a reliable stream of customer data. And so, at Harrah's headquarters, the data mining began.

In order to create a new incentive program, Harrah's computed the LTV (lifetime value) of each customer. The results were surprising—the best customers were not high rollers, but middle-aged and senior adults who had time on their hands, had comfortable incomes, and enjoyed playing the slots. Harrah's also found that satisfied customers had increased their gambling by 24% per year, while those who were unhappy decreased their yearly gambling by 10%.

Harrah's developed a number of incentive programs based on this knowledge. First, a series of direct mail communications were sent out, inviting lapsed customers to return. For example, if a customer who typically spent $1,000 per month hadn't gambled at Harrah's in a specific time frame, that customer would receive an invitation to a special event. If the same customer had lost money on his or her last visit, the event might be VERY special. Second, Harrah's implemented a three-tiered "customer care" program: Gold, Platinum, and Diamond cards were issued, based on customers' predicted LTV. Platinum and Diamond cardholders received higher levels of service, because Harrah's had realized what the best customers wanted. The article explains,

> They didn't want to wait in line to park their cars, or eat in restaurants, or check in at the front desk. So we decided to make a point of routing our customers into three different lines. People who weren't card-carrying Harrah's members and Gold customers stood in lines at the reception desk or the restaurant. Platinum customers would stand in still shorter lines, and Diamond cardholders would rarely ever have to stand in line. This created a visible differentiation in customer service.[79]

Gold customers could see that others were getting better service and so were motivated to earn higher points to move up to the Diamond service level.

Harrah's program is a great example of a relationship marketing program at the highest level. Harrah's was able to build relationships with key customers, leading to higher customer lifetime value (LTV) by

- keeping more of its customers,
- increasing the "share of wallet" of those customers, and
- decreasing the cost of doing business with them.

Data-driven print can provide a way to build those relationships through the delivery of timely and relevant offers.

DATA-DRIVEN PRINT OPTIONS WITHIN THE ASK FRAMEWORK

We have seen how customized marketing communications can be harnessed to meet the three marketing goals of the *ASK* model: acquiring, serving, and keeping customers. To summarize this model, demand generation or *acquiring* a new customer involves building awareness, inducing trial or inquiry, and motivating a customer's first purchase. This is often accomplished via mass communications to solicit leads or responses by interested prospects. After customers make an initial purchase, the *serving* function can be mediated by transactional documents that record the order itself, when it is fulfilled, and billing information. *Keeping* customers can be facilitated by customized communications that cross-sell or up-sell in order to increase share of wallet and retention.

Six categories of data-driven printed communications can be used to implement the *ASK* model. They are arranged here from the lowest level of complexity (versioning) to the highest (fully customized).

1. **Versioning:** These printed documents are varied according to groupings of individuals with a specific trait or characteristic. The printed document is not designed for a specific individual, but instead the document a person receives is determined by that person's group membership (such as geography, gender, or language). An example of this is Ace Hardware's customized advertising inserts, presented in the case study at the end of the chapter.
2. **Mail merge:** This printed document varies *only* the name, address, and salutation.
3. **Personalized printing:** Data about the recipient, beyond name and address, is used to create a more relevant offer based on demographics, lifestyle, or past buying history.
4. **Transaction printing:** These business documents (such as bills, state-

ments, orders, receipts, delivery notices, invoices, or shipping slips) speak to an individual customer. Transaction documents often include data center information printed on static or pre-printed forms.

5. **Internet on-demand:** Templates of a document are distributed by the Internet so that a number of document authors can add personalized content. This might include the name and photograph of a local dealer placed in a document template that is managed by a corporate manufacturer. Internet on-demand is often used to develop dealer-specific documents such as sales collateral.
6. **Fully-customized communications:** This sophisticated publishing technique can vary every element on each printed piece, from brochures to newsletters. Fully-customized communication enables organizations to create unique content for each recipient based on a database of information about the person.

Table 4.1 links these six options to the *ASK* marketing objectives described in this chapter.

CONCLUSION

Creating and delivering data-driven printed marketing materials is always related to a set of predetermined marketing objectives. When little or no information is known about a specific customer, an acquisition goal is appropriate, and the degree of customization will be low. When more information is known, serving and retaining the customer becomes possible. To meet this new goal, the complexity of customization in marketing materials will increase, bringing with it a need for more sophisticated database and print production technology.

Before we examine the business models that deliver customized messages (Chapter 6), we will look at the systems needed to make them work. The next chapter provides an overview of the information technology that is required to produce data-driven print at the most complex level.

Table 4.1 *Type of data-driven print and the associated* ASK *marketing objective*

TYPE OF DATA-DRIVEN PRINTED MATERIAL	*ASK* MARKETING OBJECTIVE	EXAMPLES
Versioning	ACQUIRE	One version of a gardening catalog is sent to households in the northeast and another is sent to households in the southwest.
Mail merge	ACQUIRE	A new music store buys a mailing list of local households compiled from people who subscribe to a music magazine. All households on the list get a postcard announcing the opening of the store.
Personalized printing	SERVE AND KEEP	A phone company suggests that a customer move up to a new plan based on prior calling history (this offer is not included in the billing statement). Credit card offers are sent based on a client's credit history and balances.
Transaction printing	SERVE	Mutual funds statements or bills communicate more than just monthly balances, e.g., credit card statements show the breakdown of purchases by product category in a year.
Dealer/channel partner programs using distributed printing, print-on-demand or Internet on-demand	ACQUIRE AND KEEP	Dealer-specific documents are produced with help from the corporate infrastructure, such as sales collateral or store-specific offers. For example, custom-printed menus allow a franchise owner to select which desserts to offer.
Fully-customized communications	KEEP	A customized mailing is created based on past purchases and predictions of what new needs for similar or related items will arise. For example, information about a new model of a leased car is sent to those whose lease is expiring soon.

CASE STUDY4.1: BILLS CAN BRING MORE THAN JUST HEADACHES: USING MONTHLY STATEMENTS AS VITAL COMMUNICATION TOOLS

by Barbara A. Pellow, *Digital Output*, February 2004
Reprinted with permission of *Digital Output* magazine,
http://www.digitaloutput.net

Billing statements are the one guaranteed communication that gets opened by the recipient every month. Bills have not always been viewed as an important marketing communications tool and were typically deemed documents that rendered accounting information about transactions between the parent company and its customer. In today's frenzied environment, the billing statement is taking on a new importance as a clear, concise, and valuable communications tool. To retain current customers, cross sell customers on new products and services, and manage customer service costs, creative marketers are looking at the statement as a critical vehicle for marketing communications.

THE VALUE OF A STATEMENT

DST Output, a subsidiary of DST Systems Inc., is working with its customer base to help them leverage their billing statements as marketing tools. DST used to be viewed as a billing statement print and mail supplier, but the company is now focused on the ability to create personalized communications that connect corporations with their customers.

DST Output is the largest first class mailer in the U.S., with three mega-production centers in El Dorado Hills, California; Hartford, Connecticut; and Kansas City, Kansas. The company controls more than 1.5 million square feet of production space. Its 3,000+ associates produce more than 9 billon images annually and 1.8 billion mail pieces, representing nearly 2 percent of U.S. Postal Service First Class mail volumes. In 2003, DST produced more than 12 million full color digital images. In addition, DST loaded more than 183 million e-statements and processed more than $800 million in electronic payments.

THE DOCUMENT TRANSFORMATION

DST Output is a market leader in statement production in five key industry segments including cable, telecommunications, insurance, healthcare, and financial services. According to Wes Ervin, media and public relations manager, DST's view on the market segments is one of convergence. Historically, major corporations sent their customers transaction documents (statements), direct mail (promotional material) and general customer communications (newsletters and information). Ervin stated, "These were viewed as very distinct document types with very different functions. But today we are seeing convergence in these three functions. The lines are blurring and the barriers are breaking down."

THE DRIVERS OF CHANGE

The rationale for change is four-fold. First, in the face of 2003's challenging economy, corporate marketing budgets were slashed. Additionally, when it comes to customer communications, postal expenses are a major component. To the extent that a single document can be used for marketing, education and communication without changes in service level, there is a significant opportunity for corporate cost reduction.

Secondly, statements can be used as a front-line customer service tool. From changes in the trash pick-up schedule to hours of service over the holidays, the statement offers a tremendous consistent communication opportunity to reduce call center activity and associated support costs. Because the information is communicated in the document that is actually opened by the customer, the call center can focus on providing real service as opposed to dealing with customer irritation due to service changes that the customer neglected to read about in a separate direct mail piece or newsletter. The statement can also be used as an educational vehicle incorporating charts and graphs that explain usage patterns. This further reduces reliance on the support centers.

Third, corporations know that the statement is a document that the recipient opens. Traditional direct mail has a 1–2 percent response rate according to the Direct Marketing Association. Statements require action and recipient attention. Effective white space utilization on a statement for a new offer can trigger an improved response rate that increases sales, improves retention or enhances service.

Fourth, color is a big driver of change in the statement market. Historically, there were two barriers to the rapid spread of color in the billing and statement market. The cost was too high relative to lithographic printing and monochrome digital printing. And the quality was marginal. According to Ervin, "These issues have been addressed. DST Output is currently producing cost-effective, high volume full color applications using a blend of technology. We have Xerox iGen3 units, Scitex Versamark equipment and spot color Océ equipment. These devices offer color quality and affordability that would not have been feasible even two or three years ago."

AN APPLICATION EXAMPLE

Ervin shared a specific example from a leader in the defined-contribution retirement planning industry. This firm worked with DST Output to converge a traditional litho newsletter with the quarterly transactional document. In the past, the company produced a quarterly statement, printed in monochrome on plain white paper that averaged 9–12 pages. The statement-production environment did not support messaging on the statements. In addition, the company produced two quarterly newsletters: one for plan sponsors, and another for plan participants. The newsletters help investors better understand the financial markets, the risks and rewards associated with various investment choices, and so forth. They were litho printed and mailed in bulk to plan sponsors, who in turn, at their discretion, distributed the newsletter to individual plan participants. Most newsletters were four pages; sometimes they were as many as eight pages. There was no customization—all plan participants received the exact same document.

The company re-evaluated the system. The statement was redesigned as a full color application and streamlined to a two-page summary. This shorter version summarizes key information, emphasizes the results using full-color charts and coding schemes, and then adds messages to help plan participants make informed decisions about their investments. The four- to eight-page litho-printed newsletter was transformed into a two-page digital version. Those two pages became pages three and four of the new communication. The key difference is that content is no longer static—the digital content can be versioned according to plan type. The content can be personalized. And the final major benefit was that the new statement-newsletter combo weighs less than an ounce.

Ervin said, "The real benefit for the client was more for less. The cost of litho printing, shipping, processing and distributing of the newsletter was eliminated. Postage was almost cut in half since the new combo mails at less than an ounce. The call center volume has been reduced, resulting in shorter wait times and elimination of the need to add staff. And finally, the cost of full color digital printing is more on a per-image or per-page basis, however, the page count has been cut in half on average."

TECHNOLOGY LEADERSHIP

DST has worked to build the right blend of printing technology to deliver custom communications. They have historically been a leader in investment in digital black-and-white technology. The company is extending its color investment and incorporating effective utilization of both spot and full production digital color. Océ VarioPrint technology is used for 401K-type programs or a bill where the amount due is printed in a different color. The Xerox iGen3 is used for full color. Over time, Ervin's view is that as applications are re-engineered, production variable data digital color will cannibalize some portion of litho production. DST Output also has high speed Scitex Versamark equipment for advertising and direct mailers, and for imaging content on credit card statements. According to Ervin, "The use of digital color is not considered separately, but rather, evaluated in conjunction with the added value of relevant personalization." That means that DST needed to put in place the right software infrastructure to effectively utilize digital color equipment.

Extreme Dialogue is DST's primary software composition engine for a number of variable data applications. Sefas software is used for a portion of the direct mail applications, and, based on its presence in the insurance industry, DST also has an alliance with Document Sciences.

Most importantly, the company has developed a program internally called Campaign Manager that lets clients customize messaging. Campaign Manager gives clients the ability to effectively create, coordinate and manage their communications, including defining audiences, creating targeted messages, selecting or developing inserts, and scheduling campaigns that coincide with and reinforce other marketing initiatives, right from the user's desktop computer. Campaign Manager's rule-building engine allows clients to select from a variety of data elements to create simple or complex target groups, which enables them to hone in on the precise customers they need to reach, with exactly the right message.

THE FUTURE

Marketers are looking for retention, loyalty and more revenue per customer. DST Output is focused on producing a new breed of bills...to help clients leverage digital technology and gain marketing advantage without incurring incremental costs. DST plans to support clients by mining data and building better business communications in a document that the end customer is going to open and read. DST is presenting itself to the market as the integrator for cost effective communications and has invested in the people, processes and technology to ensure success.

CASE STUDY 4.2: ACE HARDWARE INSERT TEST PASSES WITH FLYING COLORS

by Melissa Campanelli, *DM News*, November 15, 2004, Volume 26, No. 43

Thanks to a test insert program targeting a new consumer segment in May, Ace Hardware's Chicago area stores saw paint and paint supply sales climb 24 percent compared with the same period in 2003.

The 4,800-store wholesale cooperative generally relies heavily on inserts because "they are cost effective," said Colleen Donahugh, print, production and co-op manager at Ace Hardware, Oak Park, IL. "Inserts have a very broad reach at a very low price per impression."

Ace decided earlier this year that it needed help testing the effectiveness of its ad insert program and also wanted to test new customer segments. After consulting with Vertis, it decided on test targeting its newspaper inserts using psychographic data. Vertis, Baltimore, prints more than 40 percent of the 575 million inserts Ace distributes annually.

This was unusual because normally with insert advertising, "demographics and psychographics are not involved," Donahugh said. The ZIP codes surrounding a store usually form the basis of an insert program.

To find the appropriate new consumer to target, Vertis used the research from its annual customer focus study, which tracks consumer behavior across industry segments such as home improvement, furniture, grocery, sporting goods and home electronics as well as media that include ad inserts, direct marketing and the Internet.

Vertis then analyzed those groups in its RISC AmeriScan, which uses a personality segmentation system to analyze the sociodynamic profiles of respondents. Vertis found an untapped consumer segment that would be attracted to retail destinations offering home decorating solutions. The market was "slightly younger and more affluent than Ace's core customer, who tends to be middle class, middle income and slightly older," Donahugh said.

The insert test targeted both groups: 40 percent of the roughly 2.5 million inserts went to Ace's core customers while 60 percent went to the new target.

Vertis then looked at newspaper zones and chose those with the highest potential for the core customers and for the new targets. Ace focused on the Chicago market, its largest U.S. market, with 155 retail stores. Newspapers used were the *Chicago Tribune* and *Chicago Sun-Times*, along with their networks of suburban papers.

Ace used different inserts for each segment. Both aimed to spur paint sales. They were designed to get customers into retail stores May 14–17. Identical products were highlighted, and both were eight-page inserts, but each had a different creative execution.

"The core customer responds to price, product and value, so their cover was a screaming deal of 'Buy 2, get 1 Free!' which really emphasized the free offer," Donahugh said "The other group, however, responds more to an idea that 'these are the types of things that I can do,' and had a woman on the front cover painting a wall.'

The color palette in each insert differed for each target group, she said.

"The core customer responds to stronger colors while the new target responds to softer, more trendy colors, so those are the color schemes we chose for each group," she said.

Donahue attributed the bulk of the results to the new target group.

"I think we connected with a target audience that generally looks to Ace as a place where they would shop for their paint and supplies," she said.

"I think they think of us as a hardware store, and not necessarily when they are thinking of home décor."

55. Kotler, *Marketing Management*.
56. Treacy and Wiersema, *The Discipline Of Market Leaders*.
57. Kotler, *Marketing Management*.
58. Direct Marketing Association, *The State of Postal and E-Mail Marketing*.
59. Ibid.
60. Peppers, "Jaguar Uses Mass Market to Learn About Individual Customers," *http://www.1to1.com/View.aspx?DocID=28658.*
61. Pellow, Pletka and Banis, *Investing in Digital Color...The Bottom Line*, (PICRM-2003-10).
62. Six sigma was the name of the quality program developed at Motorola in the 1980s to reduce defects in production. See *http://www.isixsigma.com/library/content/c020815a.asp* for more on the history of six sigma programs.
63. Rust, Zeimthal, and Lemon, *Driving Customer Equity.*
64. Sorce and Edwards, "Defining Business-to-Consumer Relationships."
65. Bagozzi, "Toward a Formal Theory of Marketing Exchange."
66. Coviello, et al., "How Firms Relate to Their Markets."
67. O'Malley and Tynan, "Relationship Marketing in Consumer Markets."
68. See the discussion of operational customer relationship management (CRM) in Peppers and Rogers, *Managing Customer Relationships.*
69. McKeon, "Looming in Early '06: A $9 Billion Hit?"
70. Reinartz and Kumar, "The Mismanagement of Customer Loyalty."
71. Reichheld, *The Loyalty Effect*.
72. Morgan and Hunt. "The Commitment-Trust Theory of Relationship Marketing."
73. Iacobucci and Hibbard, "Toward an Encompassing Theory of Business Marketing Relationships (BMRs) and Interpersonal Commercial Relationships (ICRs)."
74. Sheth and Parvatiyar, "The Evolution of Relationship Marketing."
75. Sorce and Edwards, "Defining Business-to-Consumer Relationships."
76. Pressey and Mathews, "Barriers to Relationship Marketing in Consumer Retailing."
77. Fournier, Dobscha, and Mick, "Preventing the Premature Death of Relationship Marketing."
78. Loveman, "Diamonds in the Datamine."
79. Ibid.

CHAPTER FIVE

INFORMATION TECHNOLOGY REQUIREMENTS FOR PRODUCING DATA-DRIVEN PRINT

SO FAR WE HAVE IDENTIFIED two barriers to the widespread use of customized marketing communications. The first, as we saw in Chapter 4, was not having an articulated marketing strategy in order to make the best use of the unique capabilities of digital printing technology. The second barrier, the lack of an adequate information technology infrastructure, is addressed in this chapter. We will examine the technical components a firm needs to produce data-driven print.

The major components of an information technology system that can produce customized printed materials are presented in the workflow diagram (Figure 5.1). Each component is discussed in this chapter.

DATABASE FUNDAMENTALS

The crucial starting point is the data. Often the data are provided by the client. Otherwise they are purchased or rented from list vendors who can provide a target population for a client's marketing needs. Experian, Dun & Bradstreet, and Hoover's are companies that sell or rent prospective client lists and provide demographic overlays to existing customer files.

The quality of data can make or break the success of a variable data print (VDP) application.[80] In a 2004 survey conducted by the Printing Industry Center at RIT, 80% of respondents indicated that "poor data quality" was a challenge when implementing a VDP application. Print services providers who use client-supplied internal data need to be aware of the processes the client uses to ensure data quality. These processes include data cleansing, scrubbing, and updating. Quality assurance is also a factor when buying data. When purchasing or renting data from a list vendor, an important criterion is determining how recently that data was updated. Making sure that customer

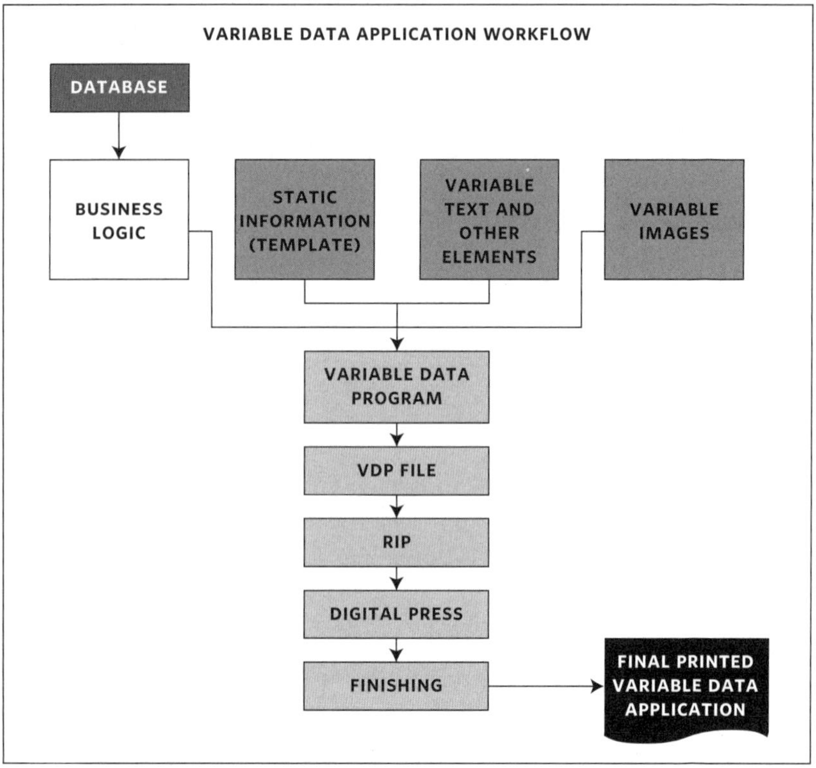

Figure 5.1 *The variable data application workflow*

data in a database are correct and accurate can be a very time-consuming and resource-intensive process.

Another element of the quality of data is *degree of specificity*. For example, if a firm has customer names but no transaction data, it will not be able to predict when or what those customers might buy again. There are two criteria that define when a database can be considered useful:

1. The database must contain all the data that are needed to execute the application successfully.
2. The database must be in a file format that the software can understand.

The nature of a firm's customer data will also determine what can be learned by *data mining*, the "iterative process of identifying previously unknown relationships and patterns in data to solve a business problem."[81] Not only must the data be accurate and specific, it must also be organized in a

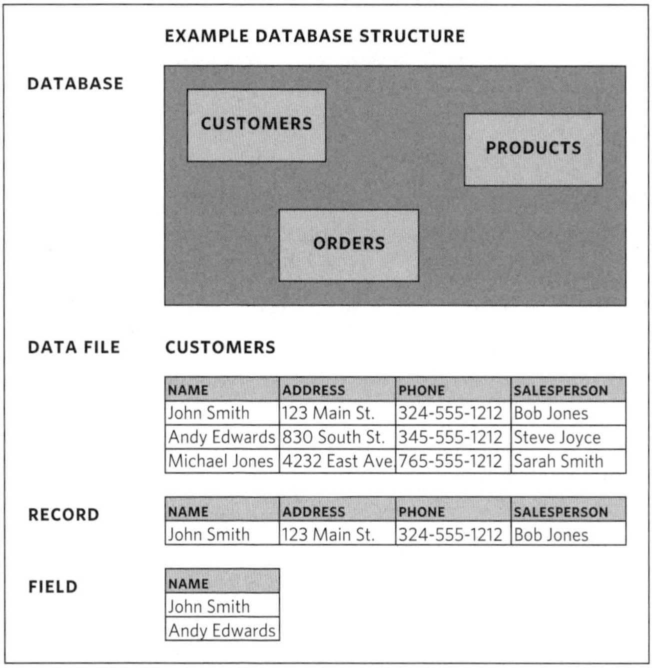

Figure 5.2 *The basic structure of a relational database*

way that can be used in common applications. The database concepts that VDP users need to understand are explained below.

COMPONENTS OF A DATABASE

There are three main objects that comprise a typical database: the *data files, records,* and *fields.*[82] A database can contain one or more data files. The data file is an entity that contains information about the objects in it. Objects inside a data file are called records. The attributes of a record are its fields. In other words, fields are the particulars of a record. If, as is pictured in Figure 5.2, records are seen as the rows of information in a data file, then the fields are the columns.

Figure 5.2 depicts a database that could be used by retailers to track customers, products, and orders. The database would contain several data files such as a file of products that the company has available for sale, a file of all of its current and past customers, and a file of the orders that those customers have placed. The data files would contain records with information about each individual customer, product, and order. In the records would be fields such as item numbers, item descriptions, order numbers, order totals, customer names, and customer shipping addresses.

ORDER

NAME	ADDRESS	PHONE	SALESPERSON	ORDERNUMBER	ORDERDATE	QUANTITY	PRODUCT	TOTALPRICE
John Smith	123 Main St.	324-555-1212	Bob Jones	12334	9/25/2003	3	Widgets	$100.87

Figure 5.3 *A single record in a data file*

Relational Databases

If more than one data file exists, as is shown in Figure 5.2, there is usually a relationship between some or all of the data files, in which case the database is called a *relational* database. A data file is one table or level of a relational database. These so-called *flat* data files are the basic building blocks of relational databases and are often simple text files or worksheets in a spreadsheet program.

Figure 5.3 shows an example of a record from a flat file database. While flat file databases are suitable for simple mailing or product lists, they are not the optimal solution for a company transaction database. Although the record in Figure 5.3 is very simple, one can imagine the problems that may arise from a database with just this type of record in a single data file. For example, there may be multiple John Smiths in the database. If a customer made repeat purchases over time, it would not be optimal to continue to add more orders on a single record. Most customer databases overcome these complications by assigning each customer a unique number. Another complicating issue in a flat file database is ease of access to information. In the record shown in Figure 5.3, the fields could easily reach 100 columns in width, making the database harder to navigate. The solution to all these quandaries is the relational database.

A relational database is actually a set of data files that are linked through the use of *primary keys*. Primary keys are special fields that can identify unique records in a data file. In the relational database in Figure 5.4, the primary keys are "CustNumber," "ProdNumber," and "OrderNumber," acting as unique identifiers for each record in their respective tables. In the bridge table, "Orders," a primary key is assigned to each order, and then the appropriate customer and product keys are entered to link the information between the tables. Other information solely related to the ordering function, such as the quantity of products ordered, can also be included in the Orders file. The relational database structure is more efficient than a flat file database since it eliminates duplicate information and maximizes data integrity through the use of unique identifiers for each record.

Even with a relational database, issues with data integrity remain a concern. Data entry errors may create multiple "customers" in the database

CUSTOMERS

CUSTNUMBER	NAME	ADDRESS	PHONE	SALESPERSON
100	John Smith	123 Main St.	324-555-1212	Bob Jones
101	Andy Edwards	830 South St.	345-555-1212	Steve Joyce
102	Michael Jones	4232 East Ave.	765-555-1212	Sarah Smith

PRODUCTS

PRODNUMBER	PRODDESC	UNITPRICE
678	Widget	$99
890	Bookmark	$20
921	Notebook	$15

ORDERS

ORDERNUMBER	CUSTNUMBER	PRODNUMBER	QUANTITY	TOTALPRICE
1233	100	678	3	$297
2356	101	890	4	$80
5487	102	921	7	$105

Figure 5.4 *Examples of data files in a relational database*

who are actually the same individual, making it difficult to determine which record contains the correct data. For example, John Smith lives at 123 Main Street, his customer number is 100, and he has placed multiple orders with the company. On one occasion, an order representative mistakenly enters him as customer number 304. The impact of this duplicate information may be insignificant, such as John later receiving two pieces of the same correspondence in the mail. However, if the error affects billing information, a bigger problem will be created.

A process called *de-duping* can help eliminate such errors in a database. De-duping evaluates records, determining which ones are most likely duplicates and should be purged from the database.[83] Firms that purchase lists from vendors and integrate them into their internal data have to be aware that some customer records will overlap. De-duping will eliminate such duplication.

With the wealth of information that can be contained in a relational database, a company can query a customer's order history and then through data mining discover insights that may lead to future marketing efforts, including what customized offers may be relevant to that customer. Matching an offer to a particular customer utilizes *conditional logic* statements in the data mining procedures, which we look at next.

A fundamental assumption in creating customized marketing communications is that different customers will receive different offers. For example, a firm may create one offer for customers who have not purchased anything in the past six months, and a different offer for customers who have made a purchase more recently. To match the offer to the customer, *conditional logic* is used.

Unfortunately there is no common language for *programming business logic* or *conditional expressions* across all variable information design programs. However, a basic understanding of computer programming is all that is needed to learn the functions. The following sections explain the most common programming functions encountered when designing variable data applications. Each example is written in Microsoft Visual Basic code and then in Microsoft Excel. Microsoft Visual Basic is one of the easiest plain-text programming languages to read and understand, and some variable data programs use codes similar to it. Microsoft Excel functions are an excellent way to test and model conditional logic without having any prior programming knowledge. Some other variable data programs create their business rules in syntax similar to this as well.

IF / THEN

The *IF statement* is the most common expression used when creating business rules in a VDP application. Its basic operation is to test for a condition, and then do one of two actions, depending on whether the test turns out to be true or false. Many other functions can also be incorporated into an *IF/THEN* example, including some which are described in the next section. In the example below, the program is testing to see what value is in the "Gender" field in a database, in order to perform some action based on that value. If the person's gender is male, the program will output the text "Mr." for that record. If not ("else"), the program will "know" that the person is a female and therefore will output "Ms."

```
Microsoft Visual Basic
IF Gender = "Male"
      THEN "Mr."
      ELSE "Ms."
END IF
```

```
Microsoft Excel
=IF(Gender="Male","Mr.","Ms.")
```

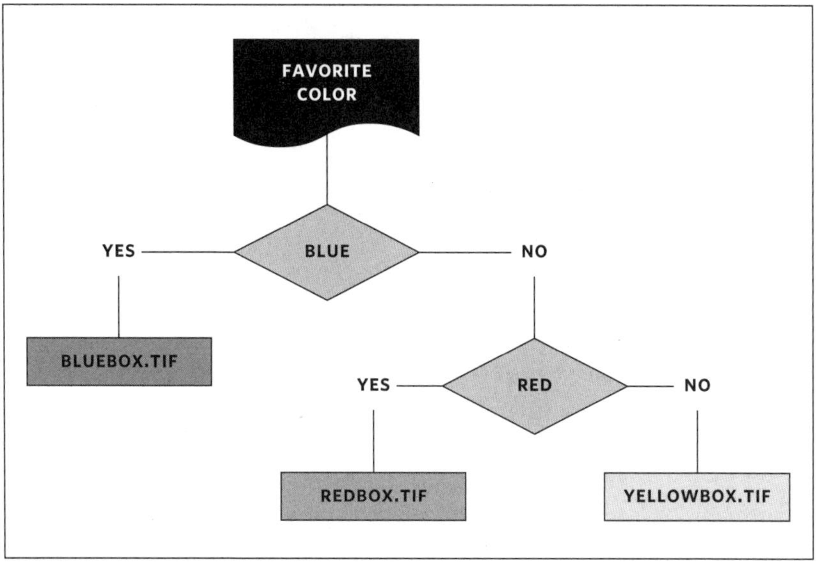

Figure 5.5 *Example flowchart of a nested IF statement*

Nested IF

A *nested IF statement* is simply one or more IF statements included within an original IF statement. This is most commonly used when there are more than two possible outcomes for a given test. For example, let's say a person's favorite color (of three choices—red, yellow, or blue) is captured and coded in a data file record. We will first test to see if the person's favorite color is blue, and if it is, the program will output the "bluebox.tif" image for that record. If not, we have to determine whether the person's favorite color is red or yellow, so we need to *nest* an IF statement within the original statement. This nested IF statement will test whether the person's favorite color is red, and if so, output the "redbox.tif" image. If the second test is also false, it is not blue or red and so must be yellow, in which case the system will output the "yellowbox.tif" image for that record. See Figure 5.5 for a flowchart of this query.

```
Microsoft Visual Basic
IF FavoriteColor = "blue"
      THEN "bluebox.tif"
      ELSEIF FavoriteColor = "red"
      THEN "redbox.tif"
      ELSE "yellowbox.tif"
END IF
```

```
Microsoft Excel
=IF(FavoriteColor="blue","bluebox.tif",IF(FavoriteCo
lor="red","redbox.tif","yellowbox.tif"))
```

AND/OR Operators

An additional way to test for multiple conditions within an IF statement is to add *AND* and *OR* operators when there are two or more characteristics that will determine the outcome. In the following example, an AND operator is used within an IF statement to test whether the record lives in a specific zip code and is at least 30 years of age. The outcome of these statements will determine the image to be embedded in the output. In our example, a specific coupon image will be output if the person described in the record is older than 29 and lives in ZIP code 44129. If the record doesn't return both tests as true, it will be considered a false value, and then a default image (e.g., a default coupon for all ages and zip codes) would be included in the output.

```
Microsoft Visual Basic
IF ZIP = "44129" AND Age > 29
      THEN "coupon1.tif"
      ELSE "coupon2.tif"
END IF
```

```
Microsoft Excel
=IF(AND(ZIP="44129",Age>29),"coupon1.tif","coupon2.
tif")
```

OR operators work in the same way that AND operators do, except only one of the two conditions in the test must be true for the statement to return a true value. In our next example, if a person's age is coded in the record as either less than 18 years old or greater than 35 years old, the person will receive the "coupon3.tif" image. A person who is between 18 and 35 years old, on the other hand, will receive the "coupon4.tif" image.

```
Microsoft Visual Basic
IF Age < 18 OR Age > 35
      THEN "coupon3.tif"
      ELSE "coupon4.tif"
END IF
```

Microsoft Excel
```
=IF(OR(Age<18,Age>35),"coupon3.tif","coupon4.tif")
```

Output Formatting / Transformations

Often the format of data in a field may not be in the appropriate format to use readily in a VDP application. For example, most dates and times in a database are stored in the mm/dd/yyyy HH:MM format. This would be acceptable for an application such as the time and date an invoice was created, but not if a firm wanted to indicate a customer's birthday. This is where a *format* function is used to convert the display of data in a field into the most useful form. In the birthday example, the format function takes the "date" field from the database and converts it into a more readable form. If the date in the database is 10/14/2005 14:23, the system will change it and output just "October 14." Each variable data program has its own unique syntax, but the concept is generally the same across applications.

Another formatting operation is called *concatenation*. When displaying information in a variable data application, it is often useful to combine, or *concatenate*, unique fields into one text string. In the example below, we are combining the FirstName, LastName, and Age fields of a record into a sentence. If the current record is John Smith and he is 34 years old, the output would read "John Smith is 34." This is a relatively easy statement to create, but the process becomes tedious if the proper spaces are not included between fields or after constant strings included in the concatenated string.

Microsoft Visual Basic
```
newString = FirstName & " " & LastName & " " & "is" &
" " & Age & "."
```

Microsoft Excel
```
=CONCATENATE(FirstName," ",LastName," ","is",
" ",Age,".")
```

These types of conditional logic statements identify the action to be taken to produce a customized offer. Depending on the complexity of the campaign, the variable elements of the communication may range from simply a name to more elaborate customization where unique graphics and text are selected. Variable information elements are combined with static elements to create the final piece. Combining the static and variable elements is further discussed below.

STATIC AND VARIABLE ELEMENTS

Once the database and business logic are prepared, the next step in creating a variable data application is the acquisition of all of the static and variable elements that will be used in the document. The static information, or the *shell* of the document, is often created in a page layout program such as QuarkXPress or Adobe InDesign. These blocks of static text and images will remain the same for each record. Examples of static elements could be a company logo, a disclaimer, or the terms and conditions for an offer.

The rest of the items in the document are variable elements, those that change depending on the record and business logic identified. Variable images can come from a number of sources, such as stock photo libraries, existing images from a company's digital asset management system, or new original images created by the company. Variable text elements can be developed by the company's marketing department, and may include headlines, sub-headlines, and body copy elements. Some variable data programs also allow the creation of data-driven charts and tables. The creator must then ensure that the correct data are available in the database to generate these graphics.

Variable text files are useful when a firm has a large amount of text that will vary with each offer. For example, the specifications related to feature products will vary when each recipient receives information about a different product. If one record needs information about "Item A" in its VDP communication, a text block with those specifications and a description of "Item A" would be used. Once all of these elements are identified and collected, they can then be incorporated into the VDP application.

VARIABLE DATA SOFTWARE PROGRAMS

Now that we have assembled the static and variable text and graphic assets to be used in our variable data application, as well as the business logic to dictate how these assets will be used with the accompanying database, we need to bring all of these elements together to create a variable data document. There are many software programs to choose from since at least 28 different vendors supply variable data creation programs.[84]

These programs vary by complexity, and some are created for specific application types. Some variable data programs are designed for creating billing statements or other transaction documents, and others are meant to create marketing collateral. In a 2004 Printing Industry Center survey, RIT researchers found that the three most common VDP software programs used by respondents were HP *Yours Truly*, Atlas Software's *PrintShop Mail,* and Creo's *Darwin Desktop.*[85] We also describe two other options in this chapter, XMPie's *PersonalEffect* and *uDirect.*

HP Yours Truly Designer[86]

Yours Truly Designer is the VDP software program offered by Hewlett-Packard for its Indigo line of production color presses. It uses the Macintosh platform and will only accept QuarkXPress design files. All data files must be in a "comma separated value" (csv) format.

The document is designed within QuarkXPress using its graphical user interface. The information that fills the text and image boxes is located in a database where it is organized into input channels defined by the columns in the database. Each channel specifies the nature of the information, and all information within the channel must be similar. For example, image files within a single column must be in the same format (e.g., JPEG). There can be static text channels, variable text channels, image channels, and file channels. To link the data to the appropriate place in the design, a text channel icon is placed in the text box; this icon points to the name of the field in the database that contains this information (e.g., First Name). For images, a similar process is used except the location is defined by the image channel icon. A variety of image files can be used including TIFF, JPEG, EPS, PDF, JLYT, and PS.

Output is defined by imposition rules. Yours Truly Designer has 16 imposition templates (e.g., business cards) to assist in the layout of the pieces on a spread. These templates optimize the paper use and deliver efficiency to the finishing operations. Or, users can design their own custom templates. The output function also allows spot colors in the design.

Output options are JLYT, PPML, or PDF. The job output files include the database file and the embedded images. Fonts in variable fields in the database must also be installed on the Indigo device. HP Indigo presses use SNAP technology to assemble the variable text or image data at full print speed without needing to RIP (raster image process) it.

Atlas Software's PrintShop Mail[87]

PrintShop Mail can accept static input from a variety of software packages, such as Adobe InDesign, Microsoft Word, and QuarkXPress. It also supports many database types, including Microsoft Excel, Microsoft Access, delimited text files, and ODBC-compliant databases. PrintShop Mail operates in both Macintosh and Windows environments.

After opening the static information and a database in PrintShop Mail, the user drags and drops text fields or image fields from the database into the design. This graphically-oriented approach allows the user to see exactly where variables are placed. For more in-depth conditional programming, the "Expression Builder" allows users to build their own business (conditional) logic. PrintShop Mail also lets users verify their own conditional database programming rules, ensuring that their variable data information will fit into the allotted variable fields.

PrintShop Mail supports all major RIP (raster image processing) technologies, including EFI FreeForm, Creo VPS, PPML/VDX, and Xerox VIPP. Because PrintShop Mail also emits PostScript and Optimized PostScript output, it can drive output to any PostScript printer. Because PrintShop Mail is relatively user-friendly and affordable, it has gained wide market acceptance. There are more than 10,000 users worldwide, including small and large corporate in-plants as well as print-for-profit establishments

Creo Darwin[88]

Like other variable data solutions, Darwin defines variable and fixed elements and sends them to the RIP. Reusable elements are ripped once and stored for future use, enabling effective and fast processing of variable documents. When purchasing the software, the user has the option of either the Desktop or Pro version. The Pro version contains all of the same features as the Desktop edition, but it also supports data-driven graphics and Web-based "hot" folders. The hot folders enable a user to create a pre-defined document, and then multiple users can upload their own databases to create campaigns for their own target audiences.

In 2005 Creo released an update to both Darwin Desktop and Darwin Pro, which supports QuarkXPress 6.5, Adobe InDesign CS, and the Mac OS X operating system. The software supports more complex and larger databases with faster processing speeds. It also includes improved on-screen previewing and proofing to let designers check for the longest record and for hidden text that exceeds box boundaries.

XMPie: PersonalEffect and uDirect

XMPie is a leading solutions provider for cross-media dynamic publishing.[89] The company's PersonalEffect software suite unites customer databases and creative content for both print and web personalized communications. Applications in the PersonalEffect suite include uPlan, uCreate, uProduce, and uGen. PersonalEffect easily integrates with large-scale databases and CRM systems.

In the uPlan application of PersonalEffect, users define the variable elements for their VDP applications by importing Microsoft Excel, Microsoft Access, or other ODBC-compliant databases. After the variable elements are defined, XMPie's ADOR technology (automatic dynamic object replacement)

creates a business logic and object definitions that can be used cross-platform without any specialized programming knowledge. uPlan then outputs a "plan file" that defines all of these elements for both print and web applications. A user can create ADOR objects for variable text, images, tables, text files, and even layers within Adobe InDesign.

uCreate, a plug-in that supports Adobe InDesign, QuarkXPress, Macromedia Dreamweaver, and Adobe GoLive, brings the ADOR objects associated with the plan file into the static information shell. The advantage to this plug-in architecture is that users can create static information in whatever environment they prefer, and then integrate the variable elements into the application. uCreate also enables live desktop proofing and copyfitting controls.

The uProduce web-based server application brings all the elements together for production. On the uProduce server, the user uploads the plan file, static and variable elements, and layout files, and can also connect to any large-scale databases or CRM systems that are being used as data sources. The user can proof the application live on screen and then generate a PostScript, PDF, VPS, VDX or VIPP file for output on a digital press. If there is a Web component to the application, the server also creates and hosts dynamic Web pages. Tracking features built into the Web server portion of uProduce enable campaign tracking and measurement for the customer.

uGen is an add-on to the uProduce server that enables the creation of Web-to-print applications. For example, with uGen a franchiser can offer customized, Internet on-demand applications for all its franchisees. uGen takes existing plan files, static and variable elements, and layout files, and then lets a user select a layout and integrate his or her database into the application to generate a print-ready file. The user can either manually type in the database information into the Web form or simply upload a database in any format that PersonalEffect supports. In our example, the franchiser defines the plan and layout files, so that the franchisee will most likely not need to wait for company approval for a customized application, which will enable quick delivery of the printed pieces.

There are several other add-on applications available to complement the PersonalEffect suite. With uImage, a plug-in for Adobe Photoshop, the user can create images with dynamic text, layers, special effects and filters. The files will still support Photoshop Smart Objects and other vector objects to maintain the images' high quality during the personalization process. Another plug-in, uChart, enables data-driven charts and graphs to be produced directly in the Adobe InDesign environment. The user has full control over the style and formatting of the charts, and can even produce 3D charts. Finally, uStore is a wizard-based add-on that enables companies to set up branded Web sites to sell variable data print applications. Companies can select document templates to be displayed on the storefront, and allow users to upload their databases and customize variable fields on the documents. The system can then process the order and send it to print.

XMPie has also released an entry-level variable data print application: uDirect. This application contains all of the basic functionality of the PersonalEffect suite, but all in one self-contained Adobe InDesign plug-in. No programming or scripting knowledge is required to use uDirect, as all conditional logic is defined in a graphical, wizard-like environment. For applications requiring advanced logic and programming, XMPie has released uDirect Professional, which includes uPlan, the same module included with the PersonalEffect suite. Here users can define advanced logic to be implemented with the uDirect InDesign plug-in. Both uDirect packages work in concert with PersonalEffect so that if a user upgrades to the PersonalEffect system, the uDirect files will be easily integrated.

VDP FILE FORMATS

Now that we have assembled all of the digital assets and combined them with the document template that was created with variable data software, the last step is to print the document on a digital press.[90] But before a job can be printed the file must first be converted to a format that will be understood by a raster image processor (RIP). A RIP is "hardware and/or software that can translate data from PostScript and other high-level languages into dots or pixels in a printer or imagesetter."[91] Files are converted to PostScript or another page description language (PDL), and then further converted by the RIP into raster format and sent to the press.

Similar to PDLs for static printing, variable data has its own set of PDLs. However, a specific RIP support must be used for specific PDL formats. When selecting a digital press and RIP, a user must confirm that the chosen variable data PDL will also be supported by the RIP. The following is an overview of three of the main VDP file formats that exist today.[92]

VPS

Creo's *Variable Print Specification* (VPS) is a popular variable data printing file format in use today. Like most VDP file formats, it is based on PostScript but has been altered in order to optimize it for variable data printing. There are many other programs that can generate VPS files, including PrintShop Mail, Pageflex MPower, and XMPie PersonalEffect and uDirect. However, VPS files can only be output through Creo Spire servers, which are available for a wide range of digital presses.

The most important feature of the VPS file format is its ability to detect elements on the page that are repeated throughout the document. These static elements are only processed once, which decreases the overall processing time of the job. The Gallop feature on Spire servers allows the press to start printing before the entire job has been processed. The press starts printing once the server has processed enough of the job to insure that the press won't print faster than the rest of the job is processed. This feature enables quick job turnaround times. Spire servers also give the user the ability to impose pages on the fly or make last-minute color corrections to variable data jobs.

PPML

Personalized Print Markup Language (PPML) is an open-source industry specification for variable data printing. It is sponsored by PODi, the Print on Demand Initiative, and virtually all major digital press and software vendors have been involved in creating and implementing this standard. PPML actually goes beyond variable data printing, and boasts of itself as a complete digital print specification. It includes the digital print ticket (DPT), a subset of JDF technology, which can incorporate digital print and variable data printing into the JDF standard.[93]

PPML is based on *XML* (Extensible Markup Language), the emerging standard for data exchange in applications from databases to Web design. Because it is based on XML, PPML can easily integrate with enterprise systems, Web services, and database applications, since each data source, and data recipient for that matter, can alter its structure. PPML also offers the same "RIP once" attribute as the VPS file format.

One recent addition to the PPML standard is the PPML Templating function. In order to automate and streamline the process of creating and producing variable data applications, this technology separates out the functions of document design, data integration, and production. Business rules and logic are created in a PPML template using Web scripting applications such as Perl. The data is gathered, usually in XML format. The template and gathered data then come together on a PPML-enabled digital front end, after which they are processed and output. Because individuals can be working on the three portions of the application simultaneously instead of in the traditional serial fashion, productivity is increased.

VIPP

Xerox's *Variable Data Intelligent PostScript Printware* (VIPP) has been the core format for variable data applications for Xerox products since its introduction in the mid-1990s. Like other file formats, such as VPS, it is based on PostScript and can therefore be programmed manually using a standard ASCII text editor. Again, like most other formats, when it comes time for print production, the digital front end will process the job efficiently by caching the static elements within the job.

VIPP applications can be produced in either *native mode* or *line mode*. In native mode, VIPP commands and markup are embedded within the data source. The two are separated during design in line mode, and then brought back together during processing. Line mode is the most common method for producing VIPP-compatible applications.

At first, VIPP required a steep learning curve because most users had very little exposure to PostScript programming. So several years after its introduction, Xerox created the VIPP *Integrated Design Environment* (IDE), a graphical user interface application which let users create variable data applications with the same visual WYSIWYG characteristics they were already familiar with. Since then, other software vendors such as Datalogics, Document Sciences, Elixir, and Lytrod Software have created products similar to the VIPP IDE, each with its own unique qualities.

Finally, to give users a proofing capability for variable information applications, Xerox developed the VIPP Thin Printer. This application brought VIPP and Acrobat Distiller together in order to create PDF files to quickly proof jobs off press. A PDF file is created at production-rated speeds and, if approved, can be directly sent to the press for production. Currently, Xerox DocuSP and the DocuColor, DocuTech, and Xerox Nuvera product lines are the only digital presses that can interface with VIPP-enabled applications.

RIPS AND DIGITAL PRESSES

As defined above, a raster image processor (RIP) translates data from PostScript and other high-level languages into dots or pixels in a printer. While RIPs and digital presses are separate elements in the variable data application workflow, they are usually sold as a bundle, and one cannot operate without the other.

When evaluating equipment for variable data printing, in addition to the RIP and digital press combination, the variable data application and its output file format are also important considerations because all of the hardware and software must be compatible. If a firm is starting from scratch, it should create a list of the criteria it desires in a VDP program. Whether the firm already owns some of the components of the system or not, these steps should be followed:

1. Given the chosen (or existing) software, determine what variable data (VDP) file formats the software will be able to output.
2. Create a list of available RIP options that will support the desired VDP file format.
3. Determine which digital presses are compatible with the selected RIPs, and then purchase the appropriate RIP and digital press combination, as well as a variable data program, if required.

This process may not be as simple as it appears, because digital presses with desirable features are often accompanied by RIPs that do not support common VDP file formats. In these cases a change in the choice of press, RIP, and/or variable data software must be made.

In Chapter 6, we will examine some of the more common press equipment and software in use today for implementing variable data print-on-demand programs.

ENDNOTES TO CHAPTER 5

80. The terms "variable data printing" (VDP) and "variable information" are used in this chapter in recognition of some printing equipment manufacturers and suppliers who have historically used this term to describe products and services that deliver data-driven printed communications.
81. Drozdenko and Drake, *Optimal Database Marketing.*
82. Rob and Coronel, *Database Systems.*
83. Drozdenko and Drake, *Optimal Database Marketing.*
84. Romano and Workman, *Variable Data Printing Software.*
85. Sorce and Pletka, *Digital Printing Success Models* (PICRM-2004-06).
86. HP Yours Truly Designer User Guide 6.5.
87. InfoTrends/CAP Ventures, *Production Workflow Solutions Product Compendium.*
88. Ibid.
89. XMPie, Inc., *http://www.xmpie.com/site/index.php.*
90. While some consider DI (direct imaging) presses to be digital, they cannot produce pages with variable, unique content. DI presses are often used for versioned documents, which we have described as

the most basic variable data application.

91. Adobe Systems, Inc., "Printing Glossary," *http://www.adobe.com/products/postscript/glossary.html.*

92. Descriptions of these file formats were taken from the Creo, PODi, and Xerox Web sites.

93. Job definition format (JDF) is the information file that contains metadata about a print job, controlling all production devices used to produce the printed piece. This will enable a purely automated workflow when the promise is realized.

CHAPTER SIX

MATCHING DIGITAL PRINTING INFRASTRUCTURE TO MARKET FOCUS

OUR FIRST FIVE CHAPTERS IDENTIFIED THE ELEMENTS that enable a firm to plan customized print communications within its marketing program. We have seen that data-driven print such as personalized direct mail, versioned catalogs, or unique sales brochures is only one part of a broader marketing communications plan that strives to achieve the business goals of a firm. These materials can be printed with a color or black-and-white inkjet printer (for addressing pre-printed versioned documents, statements, and signs), a black-and-white digital press (for correspondence), or color production press (for sales brochures, signs, and customized catalogs). The customized document is distributed by mail or other home delivery service, by its availability at specific retail locations, or by being personally handed to the targeted individual or business during a face-to-face sales interaction.

Businesses that want to customize their printed communications often work with advertising agencies or direct marketing firms to plan and create campaigns. These consultants may in turn outsource the printing to stand-alone printing services. Commercial printers with strictly offset printing equipment will have to make an investment in digital printing technology to deliver variable data printing applications. How can these businesses determine whether the investment in digital technology will pay off? And what level of investment makes sense?

The purpose of this chapter is to benchmark the innovators in digital printing to see how they have created a technology infrastructure to match their market focus. Exploratory research conducted by the Printing Industry Center in 2003[94] identified four business models related to successful digital color print services enterprises. The four models reflected different levels of investment in equipment, human resources, and telecommunications and networking infrastructures. The Center extended this research in 2004 with a quantitative study of a larger sample of digital printers, including digital print services providers, quick printers, direct marketing firms, letter shops, service bureaus, forms printers, and offset commercial printers who were venturing into digital printing.[95] This second study was designed to provide details about the financial investments required to create customized print documents, and how successful these digital printers were in selling new services to their clients.

SURVEY METHOD AND PROFILE OF RESPONDENTS

A database of 340 digital print providers had been assembled by the Printing Industry Center starting in 2001 through personal contacts and keyword searches of trade magazine press releases and articles. These digital print providers were contacted in the spring of 2004, and 171 completed a 20-minute telephone survey (a response rate of 50%).

On average, respondent firms had been in business for 35.5 years (see Figure 6.1). Thirty-one percent had started either as commercial printers or marketing agencies. A smaller number opened as service bureaus (11%) or quick printers (9%).

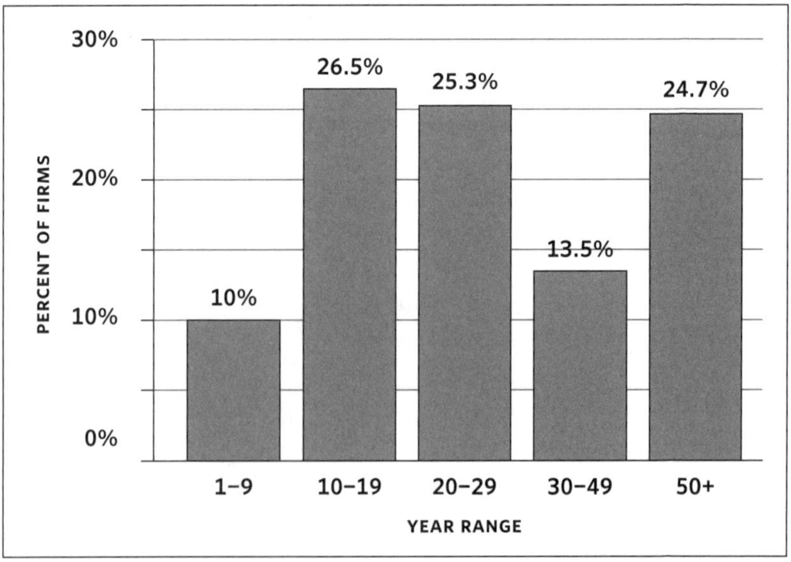

Figure 6.1 *Years firm has been in business*[96]

The size of the firms was measured in two ways—number of employees and annual revenues. A distribution of firms by number of employees is shown in Figure 6.2.

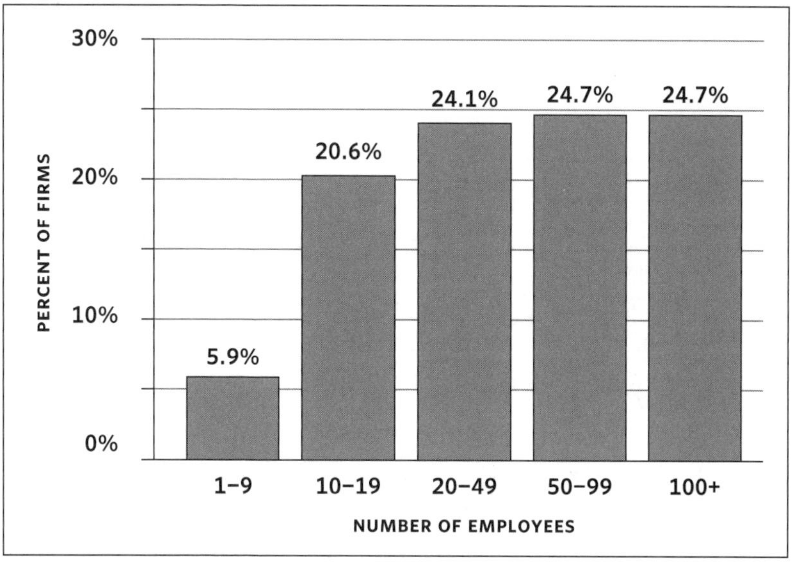

Figure 6.2 *Employee totals*

There was a median of 48 employees in the firms; the mean of 255 employees reflects the few large firms in the sample with over 3,000 employees. The average number of employees per firm by function was also calculated:

- 39 production employees,
- 13 sales employees,
- 9 customer service employees,
- 8 prepress technicians, and
- 7 information technology professionals.

In terms of annual revenues, almost one-third of firms had under $3 million in revenues (30.0%), and another third (34.1%) had over $10 million in revenues (see Figure 6.3). The median revenue growth over the previous 12-month period was reported to be 6%; the mean, influenced by a few outliers, was higher at 13%.

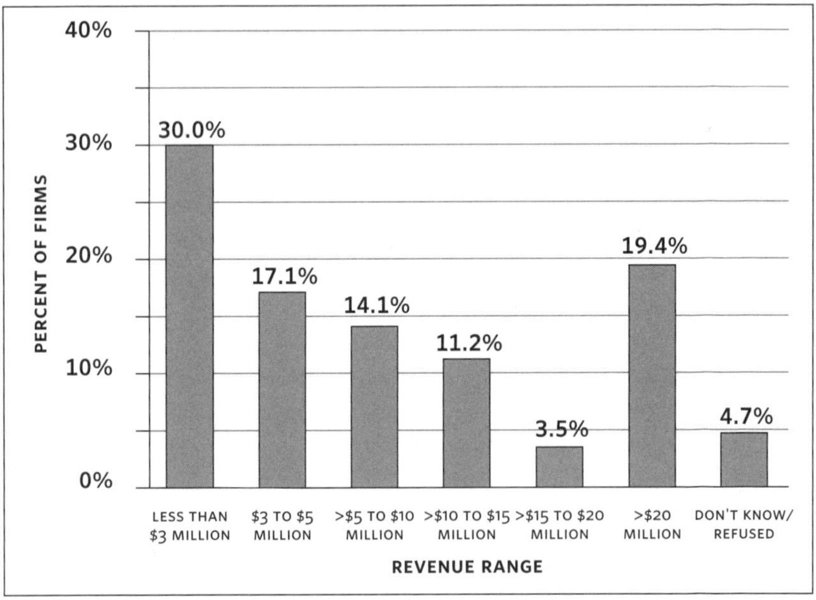

Figure 6.3 *Respondents' 2003 revenue*

Though all of these firms offer digital printing, over two-thirds (70%) also provide offset print production. Figure 6.4 shows the percent of revenue that came from variable data digital printing jobs.[97] The median was 5%, which reflects the 56% who reported that only 0–9% of their revenue came from VDP.

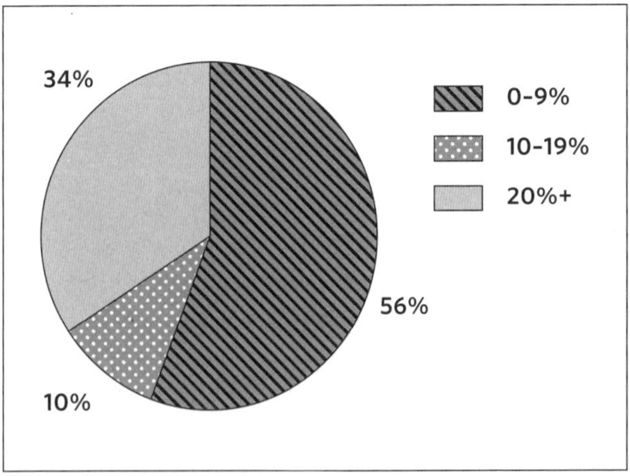

Figure 6.4 *Percent of revenue from variable data*

EQUIPMENT AND SOFTWARE

Our respondents indicated that over half (56.0%) of their *overall* digital printing is monochrome, and a somewhat lower percentage of their variable data printing is monochrome (44.8%).

The firms we surveyed used a large variety of digital printing presses. Xerox presses were installed in the greatest number of them (44.2%), followed by HP Indigo at 16.1%, and Heidelberg (now Kodak NexPress) at 10.7%. The complete list of manufacturers is presented in Table 6.1.

Table 6.1 *Frequency distribution of digital printing press manufacturers*

PRESS MANUFACTURER	NUMBER OF USERS (MULTIPLE RESPONSES ACCEPTED)
XEROX	165
HP INDIGO	60
HEIDELBERG (NOW KODAK NEXPRESS)	40
CANON	25
XEIKON	25
NEXPRESS	20
OCÉ	5
RICOH	5
IBM	3
KONICA	3
SCITEX	3
EPSON	1
MINOLTA	1

There does not appear to be a clear-cut leader for variable information software. The HP Indigo Yours Truly Designer garnered 14.6% (25/152) of responses, followed by custom-developed software (8.2%, 14/152), and Creo's Darwin Desktop (7.6%, 13/152). A complete list is presented in Table 6.2.

INVESTMENT PROFILES

The complete infrastructure investment was wide-ranging among the respondents. As measured by the 5% trimmed mean,[98] which computes a mean after eliminating outliers, the average infrastructure investment was

Table 6.2 *Frequency distribution of variable information software*

VARIABLE INFORMATION SOFTWARE	NUMBER OF USERS (OUT OF 152 RESPONDENTS)
Yours Truly Designer from HP Indigo	25
Custom-developed software	14
Darwin Desktop from Creo	13
PrintShop Mail from Atlas Software	12
Personalizer-X from TechnoDesign	11
VIPP from Xerox Corporation	10
DesignMerge Solutions from Banta Integrated Media	9
DL Formatter	9
X Data from EM Software	6
PrintNet from GMC Software Technology	5
Microsoft Word	5
Dialogue from Exstream Software	4
PlanetPress3 from Objectif Lune	3
Adobe (not specified)	3
NexTreme	2
pdfExpress from think121	2
PreS from Printsoft Americas	2
Vitesse from Elixir Technologies Corp.	2
Quark XPress from Quark, Inc.	2
FileMaker Pro	2
MPower from Pageflex	1
Persona from Pageflex	1
PersonalEffect from XMPie	1

$416,250. Table 6.3 shows the breakdown of these investments including the initial press investment, software, other hardware, and networking and telecommunications.

Most of the respondents bought their first presses between 1998 and 2002. Levels peaked in 2002, with 13.5% of firms making the investment in that year.

Table 6.3 *Investment costs for implementing VDP**

INVESTMENT COMPONENTS	5% TRIMMED MEAN
INITIAL PRESS INVESTMENT	$282,516
INITIAL SOFTWARE INVESTMENT	$17,370
ADDITIONAL HARDWARE INVESTMENT	$11,429
TOTAL ADDITIONAL SOFTWARE INVESTMENT	$14,429
TOTAL NETWORK/TELECOM/INTERNET INVESTMENT	$6,484
DATABASE INVESTMENT	$1,820
OTHER INVESTMENT	$716

**The total infrastructure investment was computed for each case and then the 5% trimmed mean was calculated on that distribution. This value was $416,250 and does not equal the sum of the separate trimmed mean investment components ($334,164) because the data used to compute the component parts means and the total investment means were not the same. That is, computations of the total infrastructure investment first added the individual component parts to calculate the total expenditures for each case. The 5% trimmed mean then eliminated the outliers on the total distribution. For the component trimmed means, the outliers for each component distribution were first eliminated and then the mean computed.*

Investment by Application

Six types of variable data applications were presented to our survey participants (see Chapter 4, Table 4.1 for a description of each). We asked whether each one of these types of applications was a major or minor contributor to VDP revenue, or whether it did not contribute at all. We also asked, "*Of the job types you indicated were a 'major' portion of the variable data jobs you print, please tell us which one represents the largest portion.*" As shown in Figure 6.5, the firms in our sample varied in the amount of work they did in each application.

Mail merge and personalized printing were major jobs for over half of the sample, and versioning was the next most frequent. Fully customized and Internet on-demand were major jobs for over one-quarter of the respondents. Transaction printing was the least frequent type of variable data job for these respondents, with 54% reporting that transaction printing did not contribute at all to company revenues.

Again, on the initial analysis of the data, box plots showed several outliers in almost each category and statistic. So the 5% trimmed mean is used again, as it was in Table 6.3, because it removes the upper and lower 2.5% of the data points and computes the mean of the remaining data. Table 6.4

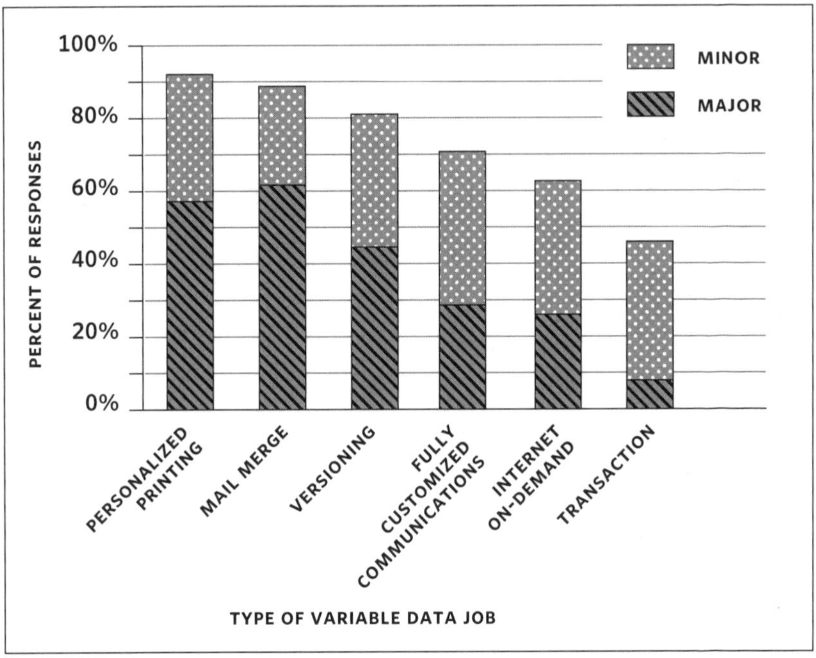

Figure 6.5 *VDP mix: Impact of each type*

summarizes our findings.

We determined two reasons why this breakdown of results did not provide a useful picture for understanding the levels of investments needed to create a successful customized printing business. First, the sample size did not yield reliable estimates since four of the six application groups had fewer than 30 firms in them. Second, all of these firms offer a number of these applications, so a simple "primary" application grouping may mask the complexity of the business models for successful digital printers. To account for the overlap in applications, a cluster analysis was performed to create a homogeneous profile of the models of digital print applications our respondents represented.

CLUSTER ANALYSIS

Using k-means clustering analysis methodology (SPSS), the firms were clustered on their responses ("major," "minor," or "not at all") to VDP application usage. The clustering solution was attempted with three-, four- and five-cluster groupings, and a four-cluster solution was found to be the most stable. Of the 171 firms entered into the cluster analysis, the four-cluster solution

Table 6.4 *Company profiles grouped by primary application (using trimmed means)*

TOTAL N = 155	VERSIONING	MAIL MERGE	PERSONALIZED PRINTING	TRANSACTION PRINTING	INTERNET ON-DEMAND	FULLY CUSTOMIZED COMMUNICATIONS
N	24	50	34	6	23	18
YEARS IN BUSINESS	24	38	42	38	26	22
2003 REVENUES (MEDIAN)	Less than $3 million	$5 to $10 million	$5 to $10 million	$5 to $10 million	$5 to $10 million	$5 to $10 million
% OF REVENUE FROM VDP	32%	8%	19%	11%	26%	22%
# OF EMPLOYEES	51	70	102	67	48	97
GROWTH IN THE LAST 12 MONTHS	10%	7%	8%	10%	25%	10%
% MONOCHROME DIGITAL PRINTING	66%	39%	59%	49%	58%	61%
% COLOR VDP	66%	39%	59%	49%	58%	61%
OWNS OFFSET EQUIPMENT	42%	82%	77%	83%	70%	61%

included all but one firm. This firm was an outlier in all three clustering attempts, and so was dropped from any further analysis. The remaining variables were then cross-tabulated by cluster and all results are summarized in the original published monograph (see *http://print.rit.edu/pubs/picrm200406.pdf*). Profiles of the four-cluster solution are discussed below. All figures represent a 5% trimmed mean unless noted otherwise.

Table 6.5 *Cluster analysis summary*

	CLUSTER 1 (N=26)	CLUSTER 2 (N=67)	CLUSTER 3 (N=46)	CLUSTER 4 (N=31)
MAJOR APPLICATIONS				
VERSIONING	4%	66%	0	100%
MAIL MERGE	19%	85%	59%	48%
PERSONALIZED PRINTING	46%	82%	43%	32%
TRANSACTION PRINTING	11%	10%	4%	6%
INTERNET ON-DEMAND	65%	41%	0	0
FULLY CUSTOMIZED	42%	51%	4%	3%
DESCRIPTIVE CHARACTERISTICS				
EMPLOYEE SIZE	70	118	51	51
PERCENT GROWTH IN REVENUES	13.2%	16.3%	11.8%	9.1%
PERCENT OF REVENUE FROM VARIABLE DATA PRINTING	23%	31%	8%	19%
PERCENT OF IT (VS. PRODUCTION) EMPLOYEES	16%	25%	7%	5%
CAPITAL EQUIPMENT INVESTMENTS				
TOTAL	$520,735	$908,833	$202,097	$309,805
INITIAL PRESS INVESTMENT	$349,402	$419,370	$171,075	$269,498
PERCENT OF PRESS INVESTMENT TO TOTAL INVESTMENT	69%	46%	85%	87%

As explained above, although the clusters were created by examining the relative concentrations of revenue from six types of variable data applications, the cluster analysis revealed four types of digital printing establishments based on application focus. This four-cluster solution, summarized in Table 6.5, revealed that versioning was a major application for 100% of the firms in Cluster 4 but for none of the firms in Cluster 3. The mail-merge application was a major source of revenue for all but Cluster 1. Personalized printing was a major source of revenue for all clusters, but transaction printing was not. Both Internet on-demand and fully-customized printing were major sources of revenue for Clusters 1 and 2 but not for Clusters 3 and 4.

The next step in the analysis was to determine whether the firm demographics and infrastructure investment also varied by cluster. The differences among clusters in their business models and investment strategies from the lowest level of investment (Level 1) to the highest level (Level 4) are described below.

INVESTMENT LEVEL 1: THE QUICK PRINT MODEL (CLUSTER 3)

Cluster 3 was comprised of 46 firms who were among the smallest of the companies we interviewed, with a mean of 51 employees. They also had the lowest amount of revenue that came from variable data printing jobs, just 8%. Their major digital printing applications were mail merge and personalized

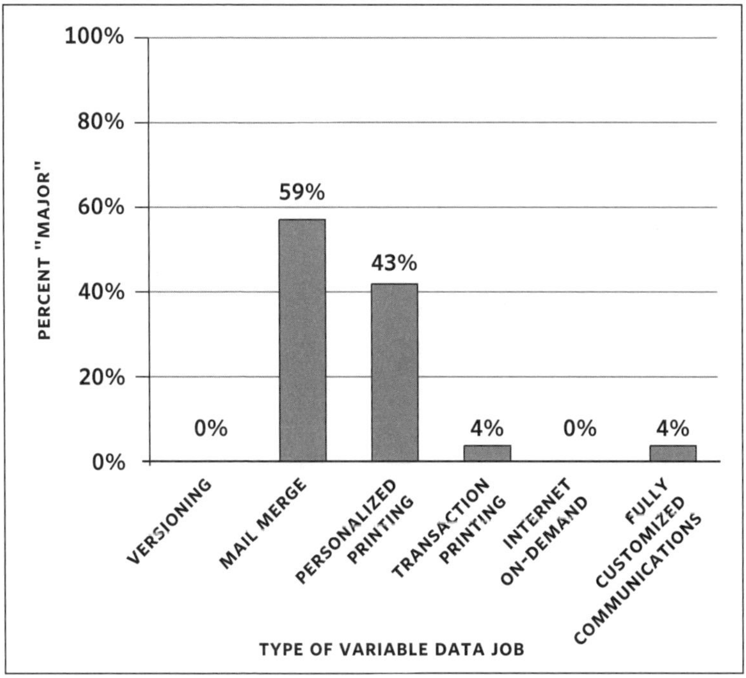

Figure 6.6 *Investment Level 1: Cluster 3—Quick print major applications*

communications (see Figure 6.6). They had made the lowest initial investment in digital presses of the four clusters (an average of $171,000), and also the lowest total investment (just over $200,000). Their average annual revenue growth was 11.8%. The percent of IT employees versus those in production was 7%. Although we decided to call this the "quick print" cluster, a majority of these firms (74%) also own offset equipment, so the quick print nomenclature may be somewhat misleading. The quick print name refers solely to their digital applications. A better label for the cluster, consistent with its application focus, might be "letter shop."

INVESTMENT LEVEL 2: THE COMMERCIAL SHORT-RUN MODEL (CLUSTER 4)

Cluster 4 was comprised of 31 firms and resembled the quick print cluster in its size (a 5% trimmed mean of 51 employees), and the ratio of IT employees to production employees (5%). However, Cluster 4 had more revenue from VDP jobs (19%) because 100% of these firms reported versioning as a major printing application. (See Figure 6.7 for a distribution of major applications.) Versioning is a common way for established commercial printers to start their foray into digital printing (by digitally printing jobs with shorter

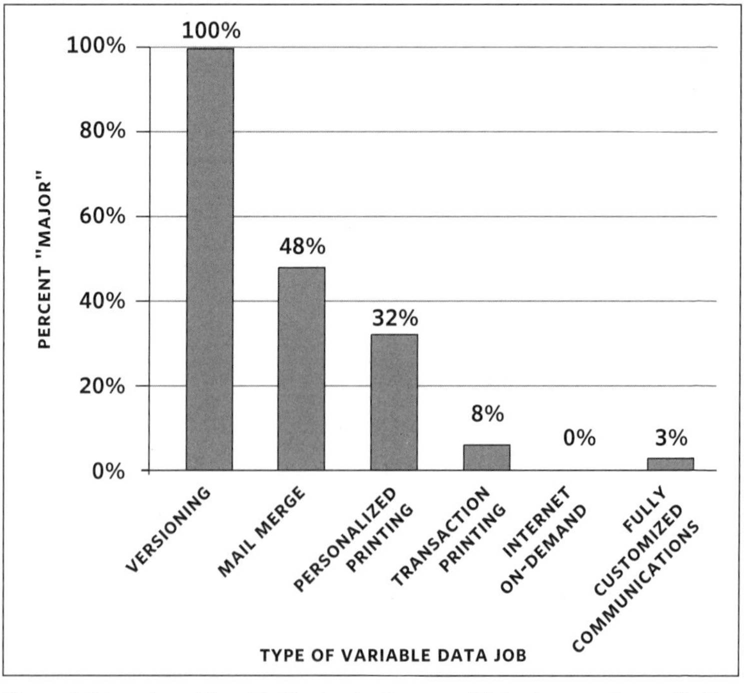

Figure 6.7 *Investment Level 2: Cluster 4—Commercial short-run major applications*

run lengths than those most often produced on offset presses), hence the name of the cluster. The average investment in presses was $269,500 and the total investment was approximately $310,000. Based on the long-term history of Cluster 4 firms, a significant infrastructure was already in place for finishing, fulfillment, and distribution. This reduced the need for additional infrastructure investments, so the primary cost for moving to VDP in Cluster 4 was largely associated with the price of the digital press equipment (87% of the original investment). The average revenue growth (trimmed mean) was 9.1%.

INVESTMENT LEVEL 3: INTERNET ON-DEMAND MODEL (CLUSTER 1)

The cluster with the third level of investment was our first cluster of 26 firms. The firms were slightly larger in size than those in Clusters 3 and 4, with an average of 70 employees, and they derived 23% of their revenues from VDP. As shown in Figure 6.8, Cluster 1 firms most frequently handled Internet on-demand (65%) and fully customized jobs (42%). Accordingly, we called this cluster "Internet on-demand." They made the second highest overall investment ($520,000), and 69% of that was for an initial press investment, at

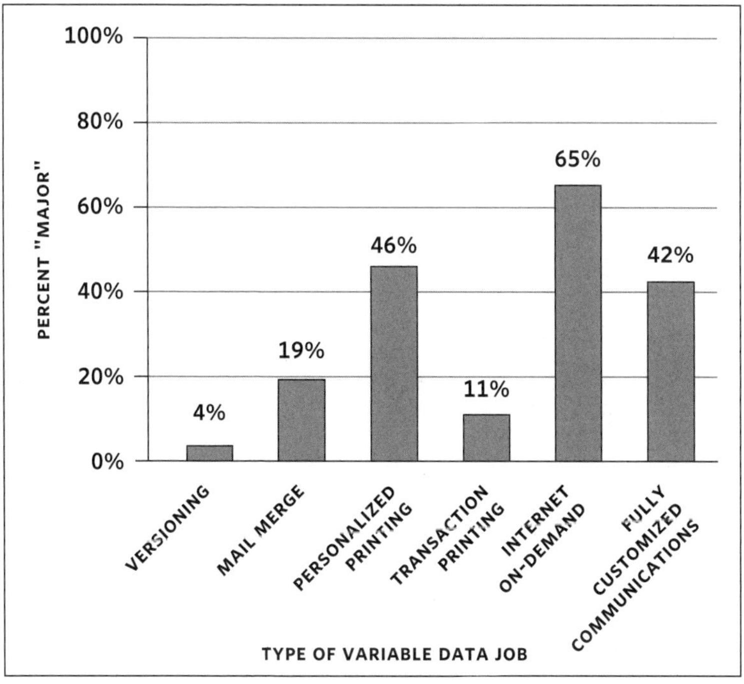

Figure 6.8 *Investment Level 3: Cluster 1—Internet on-demand major applications*

nearly $349,000. They also had a higher proportion of IT employees to production employees (16%). Their average revenue growth was 13.2%. Standard Register's DesignOnDemand application supporting Dealer Office Express (DOX) is an example of the Internet on-demand model. (See the case study presented in Chapter 1.)

INVESTMENT LEVEL 4: FULL SERVICE/FULLY CUSTOMIZED MODEL (CLUSTER 2)

The highest level of investment was found in Cluster 2. As the largest cluster with 67 firms, this group of companies also had the largest number of employees per firm, with an average of 118. The large investment in capital equipment to support digital printing reflected the large size of these companies. As shown in Figure 6.9, Cluster 2 had a major presence in almost all of the applications listed: versioning, mail merge, personalized, and fully customized jobs. We labeled this cluster "full service/fully customized." Out of an average total investment of just over $900,000 per firm, less than half (46%) was spent on digital press equipment. Revenue from VDP jobs was 31%, the highest of any cluster. The average revenue growth was also the highest reported of any cluster, 16.3%. Although only 10% of these firms

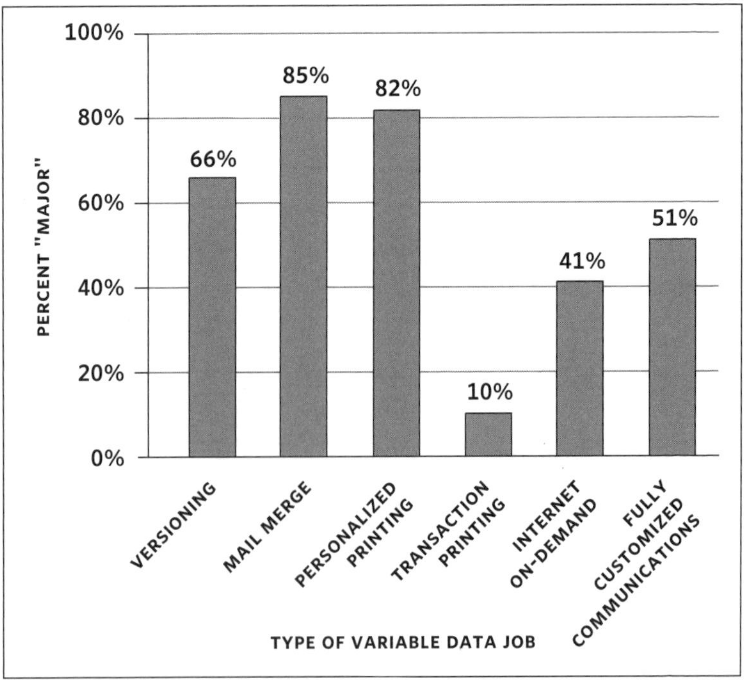

Figure 6.9 *Investment Level 4: Cluster 2—Full service/fully customized major applications*

reported that transaction printing was a major application, Cluster 2 firms still produced the most transaction printing among all the clusters.

An example of a full service/fully customized print provider is presented in the case study *Spirit of Innovation Drives R and R Images to Success* at the end of this chapter (see Case Study 6.1, p. 96).

CONCLUSION: FOUR PATHWAYS TO SUCCESS

This research confirmed and helped to refine our view of the four data-driven print business models we had identified in the 2003 exploratory study. As we found in the cluster analysis (Table 6.5), all four clusters had a 12-month increase in revenue of 9–16%. The difference in revenue growth among the clusters was not statistically significant. We can conclude that there are *many* ways of achieving business success using digital printing technology, depending on the size of the business and its traditional strengths with its client base. Entrepreneurs can get into the business with a relatively modest investment if they want to offer versioning, direct mail, or limited personalization in customized marketing communications. See the case study of Merlin International, at the end of this chapter (Case Study 6.2, p. 106), for the story of a "pure-play" digital print entrepreneur who has weathered technology and economic challenges to build a successful business over the last 10 years.

The cluster analysis presented in this chapter should not be over-interpreted to mean that there are four completely unique models. For example, there were a number of similarities between the Internet on-demand (IOD) and the full service/fully customized (FS/FC) clusters. Both had a large proportion of IT employees; both had a large proportion of revenues coming from VDP; and both had high growth in revenues. How were they different? It is likely that their differences reflect "push" versus "pull" models for personalized communications. As reported in the detailed findings of the PICRM-2004-06 monograph, the IOD group reported a higher percentage of jobs that were designed to acquire customers than the FS/FC cluster (46% for IOD and 31% for FS/FC). Conversely, FS/FC firms produced jobs designed to retain customers or build loyalty (63% for FS/FC versus 35% for IOD).

The IOD model typically uses a push strategy by targeting local franchisees affiliated with nationwide organizations in the creation of market-relevant content. In this application, a Web-based template allows a local sales channel partner to leverage its knowledge about market characteristics. The partner can add localized information (data) to an existing Web-based template to create customized marketing materials in small runs and on-demand. While the technology ensures that brand integrity and corporate messaging are not compromised, the immediate goal is to increase the number of customers coming in to a local store.

The pull strategy, on the other hand, requires a response to an action initiated by a customer. As noted in the case studies in our 2003 study, these FS/FC printers use the pull model by working with clients to plan data acquisition communications (e.g., magazine ads) to stimulate an interested customer's inquiry, directed to the firm's Web site or call center. Using variable text, pictures, graphics, and barcodes, a dynamic document is created in which the entire layout varies with the preferences captured from previous interaction with the customer. Software rules customize the content. These FS/FC printers have invested in high-speed printing technology as well as the infrastructure it requires to provide electronic distribution. This enables them to publish documents as printed pages and/or as emails, Web pages, PDF documents, SMS messages, XML files, and faxes.

As reported in *Investing in Digital Color...The Bottom Line,*[99] Salt Lake City-based Rastar Digital Marketing has used this approach to target the automotive industry with great success. The firm works with auto dealerships on both customer acquisition and retention programs. Through data mining, Rastar helps dealerships identify "high-profit" customers residing in their primary market area, and builds a communications program that reaches them one by one. Rastar produces three personalized full-color pieces over an eight-week period to drive traffic into the dealership. These communication pieces introduce the dealership to the prospect, and offer current service specials along with a special incentive to those in the market for a new vehicle. As soon as a prospect responds or comes to the dealership, he or she is immediately enrolled in a 1-to-1 marketing program. The mailings are Internet template driven, so dealerships can add unique information about their specific locations, including text, photos, and special offers. Once a prospect becomes a customer, Rastar works with the dealership on customer retention. The customer retention program incorporates service offerings and incentives for purchasing a car at the time of lease expiration or when the dealer feels the customer will be in the market for a new vehicle.

FS/FC and IOD printers can also manage the digital document supply chains of their clients. In this application, services include materials management, customized distribution, and fulfillment. The print services provider creates value by helping corporate clients to increase the efficiency of their supply chains and deliver printed materials more cost-effectively, thereby reducing inventory and loss to obsolescence. These print providers typically have roots in the traditional commercial printing market and use a blend of offset and digital equipment to produce printed products.

A word about transaction printing: only 8% of all the digital printers we surveyed reported that transaction printing was a major part of their business, and another 38% said it was a minor part. Why weren't there more transaction printers? It may be that transaction printing is concentrated among a few large printers who can produce very large volumes of mail for their customers within short time frames. An example is DST Output, the largest first-class mailer in the U.S., which produced over 1.8 billion pieces of mail in 2003, primarily for the financial services and utilities sectors[100] (see Case Study 4.1, p. 54). Another explanation may be that for smaller firms, transaction forms and billing statements are being printed in-plant. A third explanation may be due to the nature of the sample selected. Since transaction printing was one of the earliest digital applications, we may have missed transaction printers in our sample selection because we focused on those printers who had recently been in the news. Further investigation into the transaction or statement printing business is warranted.

CASE STUDY 6.1: SPIRIT OF INNOVATION DRIVES R AND R IMAGES TO SUCCESS

by Cary Sherburne, Sherburne & Associates. Excerpts from a case study prepared exclusively for the PIA/GATF Digital Printing Council, April 2004. Reproduced with permission from the PIA/GATF Digital Printing Council, Alexandria, Virginia.

BACKGROUND

In 1989, Rod Key opened R and R Images as a photographic studio in Phoenix AZ. At that time, the company operated using conventional photographic methods. As digital photography began to enter the market, Key was quick to see its value and was the first commercial studio in Phoenix to add digital to the mix. Key and his staff of 25 employees have carried that spirit of innovation through the last fourteen years, staying ahead of the technology curve—and well ahead of the pack in revenue growth. In fact, R and R Images achieved year-over-year revenue growth of a whopping 178 percent in 2003, a year that was a struggle for many businesses in the graphic arts industry.

Even as Key and his team began to benefit from the use of digital photography, the company continued to expand its portfolio of offerings, adding scanning services to augment its work in larger images and outdoor work, that, in turn, led R and R to become a full-fledged prepress service bureau, adding film and design services to its growing portfolio of capabilities. When the Heidelberg Quickmaster DI came to market in 1995, R and R saw the value of adding printing services. Continuing its practice of being an early adopter of lead-edge technologies, R and R acquired the first QMDI in Arizona, which became the foundation of its printing business. Key says, "Our strategy often put us in the position of dealing with the pain of being first to market with a new technology or service, but the upside was that we were able to establish a new business before competitors emerged." In a few short years, R and R had grown from a conventional photo studio to a full-service photo, prepress, and print business with a focus on digital services. And Key didn't stop there.

BUILDING FOR THE FUTURE

In the middle of 2002, Key determined that it was time to take a fresh look at his business. As the economy tumbled, R and R Images, like many other companies, felt the squeeze, but Key wanted to be proactive about ensuring that his company would continue to enjoy the type of success it has achieved in the past. With that goal in mind, Key engaged Mike Chiricuzio, president of Blue Moon and a former area competitor, to objectively examine what was working at R and R Images, what was not working, and how best to organize the business for the future. Chiricuzio says. "When we were competitors, our businesses were actually somewhat complementary to each other. While we both had direct-imaging presses, Rod had a very successful photo studio, and I was an early implementer of the Indigo digital offset press. Independently, we both came to the conclusion that it didn't make sense to encroach on each other's turf. After I sold my business, Rod found the idea of adding digital printing services a more attractive proposition."

The outcome of this effort was the realization that the service bureau business, which had served R and R well, was coming to the end of its life.

The competition in the DI printing marked had gotten stiffer; and a logical extension of the business—and competitive differentiator—would be the addition of a digital offset press. One of the benefits of engaging Chiricuzio in the process was that he had already lived through the implementation of digital offset printing at a time when the technology wasn't quite as stable as it is today—and he had done so successfully. Key was able to leverage those experiences as the pair put together a cohesive strategy and solid plan. The result was the installation of an HP Indigo 3000 digital press in late August 2002. The press reached profitability in only a month's time—by the end of September 2002. Chiricuzio says, "The installation hit the ground running and reached profitability faster than any other implementation I have ever seen."

R AND R IMAGES TODAY

Today, R and R Images has a sales staff of four employees who market the full range of the company's services—its photo studio, its Heidelberg Quickmaster DI, HP Indigo 3000, wide-format printing, and full array of bindery services. The company is growing at an impressive rate. In working through the business aspects of supplementing the declining service bureau revenues with revenues from a new digital printing service, the R and R team looked at a broad array of issues.

UPDATING THE IT INFRASTRUCTURE

Key also planned to make significant investments in customer-facing systems. With the rapid time to profitability for the restructured printing operation, he was able to add a programmer to his team in December of 2002 to begin the process of updating the company's IT infrastructure. To that end, Key hired Jim Lipo, whose first task was to gain an understanding of the current state of the business and work with the team to fine-tune the long-term goals. In the short-term, all of the basic infrastructure, including networks and servers, were in need of updating. In the implementation process, Key was careful to ensure that all short-term activities ultimately supported the agreed-upon long-term goals to gain the best possible benefit from all investments.

Once the basic infrastructure was updated, R and R started with some of the simpler operational improvements, including bringing the outsourced FTP services back in-house and improving its speed and functionality. The new implementation was also designed to be used from a Web browser without the need for specialized FTP software for uploading and downloading files. Key says, "Our customers have varying levels of abilities and skills. The most important thing was to make it easy and to document it well to encourage as much user self-service as possible—and finally, to assure that the proper automatic notifications were in place to eliminate the risk of unprocessed work remaining on the site."

Thus, when users visit the site to upload a file, they simply click on a button labeled "FTP," fill out a simple form, attach the file, and submit. R and R has also added an online application that allows dealers of its corporate customers to access a library of approved marketing materials. In most cases, dealers can customize designated areas of these materials (while still protecting the brand integrity of those materials), select a quantity, and pay for materials with a credit card when they order. This application was up and running within six months from the time development activity commenced and was the first online application to generate print revenue for the company.

A RATIONAL INVESTMENT STRATEGY

A key element of the plan that Key and Chiricuzio developed and deployed—and a major contributor to the success of the plan and of the company as a whole—was the rational investment strategy the company employed. For the most part, investments were funded from the existing revenues, and major investments were phased in so that each reached profitability before the next was undertaken. According to the RIT Printing Industry Center's[1] research among 66 earlier adopters of digital color printing, firms that had a well-constructed business plan that supported the level of investment required to be successful in a venture of this nature were more likely to be successful in the long term. According to the study:

---

1. *Digital Color—Where is the Market?*, by Barbara A. Pellow, Franziska Frey, Ph.D., and Patricia Sorce, Ph.D., A Research Monograph of the Printing Industry Center at RIT, September 2002 (PICRM-2002-02).

> With the market frenzy surrounding digital color, some print providers viewed the opportunity as a "field of dreams." Invite advertisers, direct mailers, and marketers, and they will come. These firms didn't develop a basic business plan that included an identified target market and an implementation plan including sales, services, and support that would yield profitability....The majority of early digital color adopters who stayed the course were not dependent on digital color as their sole source of revenue. They had other major business components that subsidized their digital color investments (p. 6-7).

Rod Key and his team, with advice from Mike Chiricuzio, followed this recipe for success, and the company's astonishing revenue growth, even in uncertain economic times, is a testament to the effectiveness of their planning and patience.

THE CUSTOMERS AND THE APPLICATIONS

One of R and R Images' long-term and very satisfied customers is TASER International. Headquartered in Scottsdale AZ, the company develops, assembles and markets less-lethal, energy-conducted weapons, primarily for use in the law enforcement, corrections, private security, and personal defense market. The company's products, commonly known as TASER "stun guns," use proprietary technology to incapacitate dangerous, combative, or high-risk subjects that may be impervious to other less-lethal means, regardless of pain tolerance, drug use, or body size—factors that the company says can cause other less-lethal options to have decreased effectiveness. The advanced TASER also has a lower injury rate than other less-lethal weapons and has had no reported long-term, adverse after-effects. The company reports that effective less-lethal weapons increase the safety of law enforcement officers, decrease suspect injuries, improve community relations, reduce litigation and police department medical and liability insurance costs, and have saved lives.

Key says, "The company's stock is up some 1,800 percent year-to-date, and we like to think that we helped them achieve that in some small way." Key states that TASER fits the profile of an ideal R and R customer.

They have a dynamic product that is needed in the current environment; they are fairly computer savvy; and they have an excellent database. According to Key, "When Rick Smith, TASER's CEO and one of its founders, saw what we could do, he understood the potential business impact immediately." The TASER database is contained within an Excel spreadsheet tool that allows the automatic calculation of the costs and benefits of implementing its solutions in a law enforcement environment, based on the number of officers the department employs. This includes the cost of the equipment, supplies and training, balanced against potential liabilities such as officer injuries and wrongful death claims. A large police department, according to TASER data, could realize savings in excess of $5 million by implementing TASER solutions.

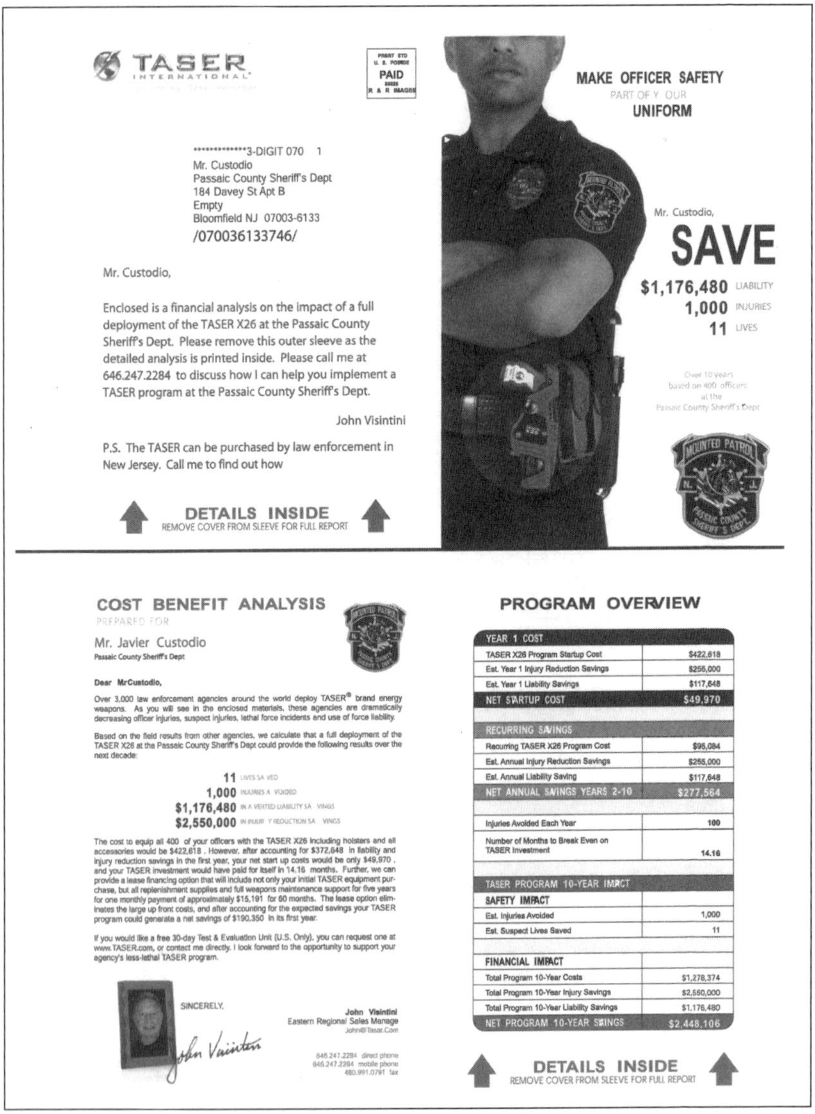

TASER INTERNATIONAL

PRSRT STD
U.S. POSTAGE
PAID
R & R IMAGES

*************3-DIGIT 070 1
Mr. Custodio
Passaic County Sheriff's Dept
184 Davey St Apt B
Empty
Bloomfield NJ 07003-6133
/070036133746/

Mr. Custodio,

Enclosed is a financial analysis on the impact of a full deployment of the TASER X26 at the Passaic County Sheriff's Dept. Please remove this outer sleeve as the detailed analysis is printed inside. Please call me at 646.247.2284 to discuss how I can help you implement a TASER program at the Passaic County Sheriff's Dept.

John Visintini

P.S. The TASER can be purchased by law enforcement in New Jersey. Call me to find out how

DETAILS INSIDE
REMOVE COVER FROM SLEEVE FOR FULL REPORT

MAKE OFFICER SAFETY
PART OF Y OUR
UNIFORM

Mr. Custodio,
SAVE
$1,176,480 LIABILITY
1,000 INJURIES
11 LIVES

Over 10 years
based on 400 officers
at the
Passaic County Sheriff's Dept

MOUNTED PATROL
PASSAIC COUNTY SHERIFF'S DEPT.

COST BENEFIT ANALYSIS
PREPARED FOR
Mr. Javier Custodio
Passaic County Sheriff's Dept

Dear MrCustodio,

Over 3,000 law enforcement agencies around the world deploy TASER® brand energy weapons. As you will see in the enclosed materials, these agencies are dramatically decreasing officer injuries, suspect injuries, lethal force incidents and use of force liability.

Based on the field results from other agencies, we calculate that a full deployment of the TASER X26 at the Passaic County Sheriff's Dept could provide the following results over the next decade:

11 LIVES SA VED
1,000 INJURIES A VOIDED
$1,176,480 IN A VERTED LIABILITY SA VINGS
$2,550,000 IN INJUR Y REDUCTION SA VINGS

The cost to equip all 400 of your officers with the TASER X26 including holsters and all accessories would be $422,618 . However, after accounting for $372,648 in liability and injury reduction savings in the first year, your net start up costs would be only $49,970 , and your TASER investment would have paid for itself in 14.16 months. Further, we can provide a lease financing option that will include not only your initial TASER equipment purchase, but all replenishment supplies and full weapons maintenance support for five years for one monthly payment of approximately $15,191 for 60 months. The lease option eliminates the large up front costs, and after accounting for the expected savings your TASER program could generate a net savings of $190,350 in its first year.

If you would like a free 30-day Test & Evaluation Unit (U.S. Only), you can request one at www.TASER.com, or contact me directly. I look forward to the opportunity to support your agency's less-lethal TASER program.

SINCERELY,

John Visintini
Eastern Regional Sales Manage
John@Tasar.Com

646.247.2284 direct phone
646.247.2284 mobile phone
480.991.0791 fax

PROGRAM OVERVIEW

YEAR 1 COST	
TASER X26 Program Startup Cost	$422,618
Est. Year 1 Injury Reduction Savings	$255,000
Est. Year 1 Liability Savings	$117,648
NET STARTUP COST	$49,970
RECURRING SAVINGS	
Recurring TASER X26 Program Cost	$95,084
Est. Annual Injury Reduction Savings	$255,000
Est. Annual Liability Saving	$117,648
NET ANNUAL SAVINGS YEARS 2-10	$277,564
Injuries Avoided Each Year	100
Number of Months to Break Even on TASER Investment	14.16
TASER PROGRAM 10-YEAR IMPACT	
SAFETY IMPACT	
Est. Injuries Avoided	1,000
Est. Suspect Lives Saved	11
FINANCIAL IMPACT	
Total Program 10-Year Costs	$1,278,374
Total Program 10-Year Injury Savings	$2,550,000
Total Program 10-Year Liability Savings	$1,176,480
NET PROGRAM 10-YEAR SAVINGS	$2,448,106

DETAILS INSIDE
REMOVE COVER FROM SLEEVE FOR FULL REPORT

Figure 6.10 *Taser variable data marketing mail piece, page 1*

Smith was attracted to the ability R and R offered to dynamically vary the data and images based on the Excel database, creating compelling, customized materials for law enforcement departments and other potential customers.

Key says, "We printed 12,000 sheets of a 100 percent variable campaign for TASER that contained over 60 variable points. The piece contained

I. PROGRAM COST

OPTION 1: PURCHASE

YEAR 1 EQUIPMENT PURCHASE			
DESCRIPTION	QUANTITY	PRICE	TOTAL
TASER X26 (# 26000)	37	$799.95	$29,598
Extended XDPM (# 26701)	37	$34.95	$1,293
Dual Cartridge Holster (# 26802)	37	$19.95	$738
Training Cartridges - 15 ft. (# 34200)	148	$16.97	$2,512
21 ft. Field Cartridges (# 44200)	111	$18.97	$2,106
Sim / Training Cartridges (# 44205)	37	$17.97	$665
XP Cartridges (# 44201)	74	$21.97	$1,626
USB X-Dataport Kit (# 26500)	4	$149.95	$600
TOTAL YEAR 1 COST			$39,137

ANNUAL RECURRING PURCHASES (YEAR 2-5)			
DESCRIPTION	QUANTITY	PRICE	TOTAL
Training Cartridges - 15 ft. (# 34200)	74	$16.97	$1,256
21 ft. Field Cartridges (# 44200)	111	$18.97	$2,106
Sim / Training Cartridges (# 44205)	37	$17.97	$665
XP Cartridges (# 44201)	74	$21.97	$1,626
XDPM with 1-year ext. warranty	37	$84.95	$3,143
TOTAL ANNUAL RECURRING COST			$8,795

OPTION 2: LEASE

60 MONTHLY PAYMENTS (estimated*)	1,406

Lease includes initial purchase and the four annual equipment purchases as outlined in option 1 Ñ all rolled into one monthly payment. **At the end of the lease, you can purchase and own all of the equipment for $1.00.**

* Payments are estimated. Contact us for firm rate quote.

III. LIABILITY SAVINGS: $10,882 / yr

Based upon field data from the Los Angeles Sheriff's Department (LASD), we believe the full deployment of the ADVANCED TASER at the Milledgeville Police Dept could avert approximately $10,882 per year in liability settlements. This is based upon an estimate from a study at LASD, using comparative analysis of liability settlements related to lethal use of force prior to their ADVANCED TASER program, and high profile uses that the ADVANCED TASER successfully brought under control without lethal force. The study estimated that LASD may have avoided $2.5 million in liability with the ADVANCED TASER in the first year of deployment. Below, we calculated the savings in liability to be $294.12 per officer per year for the LASD. Proportionately, a similar savings in liability for the Milledgeville Police Dept would yield $10,882 in savings each year.

LOS ANGELES SHERIFF'S DEPARTMENT	
Number of Officers	8,500
Total Estimated Savings for Department	$2,500,000
ESTIMATED SAVINGS PER OFFICER	$294.12

ESTIMATE	
Number of Officers	37
Estimated Savings Per Officer	$294.12
TOTAL ESTIMATED USE OF FORCE LIABILITY SAVINGS	$10,882

MORE TASER RESULTS...

PHOENIX PD

LETHAL FORCE DOWN 50%

DENVER PD

SUSPECT INJURIES DOWN 89%

The results from police departments outlined in this report were obtained with deployment of the ADVANCED TASER M26. However, given the similar operating characteristics we believe this data applies equally to the newer TASER X26.

TASER®, ADVANCED TASER®, X26, Shaped Pulse, and the Globe Lightning Bolt Logo are trademarks of TASER International. Patents: U.S. #5,771,683 and others pending U.S. and Worldwide. © 2003, TASER International, Inc.

II. INJURY SAVINGS: $30,500 / yr

In Orange County, Florida, deployment of the TASER has lead to a reduction of deputy injuries by 80%. A similar injury reduction at Milledgeville Police Dept would avoid 4 officer injuries each year, saving the department $20,000 annually in workers compensation, lost labor hours, and medical costs (assuming an average injury cost of only $5,000). Far more important than the dollar savings is the improvement of officer safety and improved morale.

ACTUAL DATA: ORANGE COUNTY SHERIFF'S OFFICE, FLORIDA	
Number of Officers	1,305
Number of Officer Injuries Per Year Before TASER	120
Number of Officer Injuries Per Year After TASER	24
REDUCTION IN OFFICER INJURIES	80%

ESTIMATE: Milledgeville Police Dept	
Number of Officers	37
Number of Officer Injuries Per Year Before TASER (est.)	4
Reduction in Injuries Per Year (est.)	4
Estimated Cost Per Injury	$5,000
ANNUAL OFFICER INJURY SAVINGS	$20,000

During its six month trial period, the Phoenix Police DepartmentÕs suspect injury rates fell by 67% - from 82 injuries per 100 force incidents before the TASER to only 27 injuries per 100 force incidents after the TASER deployment. Assuming that the Milledgeville Police Dept has a similar experience, a TASER X26 program could save 7 suspect injuries each year. In many cities, the police department may be billed for expenses associated with suspects in custody. Further, in cities where this is not the case, many suspects requiring medical attention do not have medical insurance, and the net costs of emergency room care are borne by the city or county. Assuming an average cost of $1,500 per suspect injury, the Milledgeville Police Dept could experience a cost savings of $10,500 in reduced suspect injuries.

ACTUAL DATA: PHOENIX POLICE DEPARTMENT	
Number of Officers	2,700
Number of Suspect Injuries Per Year Before TASER	690
Number of Suspect Injuries Per Year After TASER	228
REDUCTION IN SUSPECT INJURIES	67%

ESTIMATE: Milledgeville Police Dept	
Number of Officers	37
Number of Suspect Injuries Per Year Before TASER (est.)	10
Reduction in Suspect Injuries Per Year (est.)	7
Estimated Cost Per Injury	$1,500
ANNUAL SUSPECT INJURY SAVINGS	$10,500

TOTAL ANNUAL INJURY SAVINGS (estimated*)	$30,500

TASER X26

OPTIONS AND ACCESSORIES

All DPMs are rated at 300 firings at room temperature (20Í C)
All XDPMs can hold a spare cartridge and are rated at 300 firings at room temperature (20Í C)

Figure 6.10 *Taser variable data marketing mail piece, page 2* a perforated reply card, was folded to fit into a DVD case, and was mailed with a TASER product DVD. TASER was able to confirm that—as a direct result of that campaign—their sales were up 20 percent in the first quarter, and the number of prospects was up 40 percent. All of a sudden, the price of the printed piece wasn't the key decision criteria."

R and R is using the Quickmaster DI to produce TASER data sheets and TASER has also worked with R and R to create personalized invitations for trade show attendees that sets a specific time for the attendee to visit the TASER booth.

With the launch of a new product line, TASER is creating another variable campaign, this time consisting of 26,000 sheets and 120 points of variable data. As of this writing, the campaign had completed its testing phase and was ready for production in January 2004. Key says, "With double the variable-data points, we exceeded the capacity of Excel and had to convert the information to Microsoft Access."

One of the data points in TASER's database that has actually turned into an interesting selling point is the law enforcement department's emblem or logo. If the emblem is included in the department's database, it is included on all mailing to that department. As the police chiefs interacted with each other and shared information, those departments whose emblems were not included in the mailings were actually contacting TASER and offering to send the logos for inclusion in the next mailings. TASER is working with R and R to develop a custom Web site so that police chiefs can access their particular information, update it, upload emblems, and request specific information. The Web site will be live in conjunction with the January mailing.

A number of police chiefs have informed TASER that the materials they receive are so complete and compelling that they comprise a key part of the chiefs' presentation to city councils when seeking funding for TASER gear.

TASER even plans to offer the police chiefs the ability to enter online the names of city council members so that customized pieces can be mailed directly to them. Key says, "When TASER closes a deal, it represents significant revenues, often in the range of $1 million per deal. With the type of response rates we have been able to deliver, the value proposition for TASER is clear." R and R will be working with TASER to further develop online capabilities with a goal of putting all TASER materials in an online catalog. Key says, "Having this capability available for both TASER and its customers removes us even further from the commodity playing field. We are educating them on the positive impact that just-in-time printing can have on the bottom line, even for static data sheets that we produce on the Heidelberg Quickmaster DI."

HYBRID PRINTING FOR IMPROVED COST AND PRODUCTIVITY

For TASER and other customers, R and R uses a blend of its QMDI and HP Indigo presses to produce hybrid pieces. He comments, "For a number of our customers, we print one side of a piece on the Heidelberg and the other on the Indigo. This brings the price point down to make pieces more cost effective and allows our customers to harness the power of variable data at a lower price point." A common application he describes is a run of 15,000, 8.5 x 5.5-inch postcards that all have the same front. On the back, 8,000 of the cards have the same message and no addressing, and the balance have a different image with addressing. For an application like this, R and R would run 3,750 four-up sheets on the Heidelberg and then run the sheets through the Indigo to produce variable information on the reserve side. Key says, "by using both the Heidelberg and the Indigo to produce this job, we can save the clients as much as $400 to $500 on the job. While we don't sell on price, we do try to save the clients money. We see at least two or three of these jobs a week." Key indicates that he typically prints volumes greater than 500 on the Heidelberg. If the Indigo is backlogged, even runs of less than 500 might be produced on the Heidelberg QMDI. In this way, he is leveraging the blend of the two types of equipment for maximum utilization. According to Key, the customers are less interested in which press produces their work than they are in the turnaround time and the overall cost and quality of the piece.

VARIABLE EDUCATION STILL A MUST

Key indicates that although R and R is heavily selling variable-print capabilities, many of the jobs the company receives are still simply mail-merge type applications, or quite often simply addressing, which he categorizes as "the lowest form of variable data printing." In order to produce this type of work economically, Key says, a run of 10,000 sheets will be printed on both sides of the QMDI, with a single color overprint of the address applied using the Indigo. In the case of the one recent job consisting of 27,000 sheets, one side was produced on the Heidelberg while the variable side was produced on the Indigo.

Key points out, "When you are talking about runs at that quantity, it can be a huge savings for the customer—as much as a $5,000 difference over printing the entire job on the Indigo. He says, "The applications and requirements will vary by industry. For example, in health care, the client may not want to produce variable pieces. But they might need 100 brochures in Spanish about preventing heart attacks; 1,000 of the same pieces in English; and perhaps different versions for Phoenix and Tempe."

CUSTOMER DATABASES STILL A CHALLENGE

The other issue Key and his team run into all the time is the poor quality of customer databases. Many, he says, contain nothing more than first and last name and address. In those situations, R and R works with the customer to produce a multipart campaign, which consists of a generic piece addressed to the individual giving a personal URL that the recipient is encouraged to visit. The personal URL will contain additional information and offer the recipient the opportunity—sometimes tied to an incentive—to provide additional information. In this way, subsequent campaigns can be increasingly personalized, and the personal URL can be fine-tuned as well. As an added value, R and R tracks responses and reports results back to the client in a closed-loop process.

WALKING THE TALK

R and R is using personal URLs in its own direct-mail campaigns, focusing on the acquisition of email addresses and offering a free gift to those who sign up. Key says, "We know what time someone hits the site, and we are designing a tool to find out how many times people go to the site, who doesn't go to the site, and when they do go to the site, whether they take advantage of the case studies and/or answer the questions. We can generate a report that documents activities day by day.

"Our goal is to have a digital dashboard for our own business that allows us to see exactly what is happening with a given campaign. That allows us to establish a set of business rules that will trigger certain responses—such as sending a sales rep out, sending an email, or sending information about digital photography—based on the activities that occur during a particular site visit." Key cites the work HP and other equipment manufactures have done to educate equipment buyers about the types of services they should be offering to customers to help those customers grow their businesses. He has taken it a step further, however. Key says, "I want to grow as well; why can't I use these tools on my own business? And it makes me more credible when I approach customers because we practice what we preach." Thus, all of R and R's sales materials are printed on a custom basis for its own customers, and the company is tracking all results.

SUMMARY

"Our roots are in the photography business," says Key. "We were easily able to leverage our photographic heritage into printing when we acquired the Heidelberg Quickmaster DI, especially with our digital photography experience.

We knew a lot about color, and customer requirements for speed, quality, and service were well understood. The QMDI was an ideal next step for us because of its high quality and ease of operation, and it made sense to follow that with implementation of the HP Indigo and wide-format solutions to expand our portfolio of offerings." Rod Key and his team at R and R Images represent a new breed of print services providers. They enter the printing industry with a fresh perspective and few preconceived idea about how to run the business. They perform a careful business and market analysis, tap experience resources for advice and counsel, and build a rational implementation plan primarily funded from existing business revenues. And they carefully select and train sales resources to carry their message to the market. The success of this approach is validated by the company's performance of 178 percent year-over-year revenue growth and its portfolio of delighted customers, who, together with R and R, continue to push the limits of current technology and reap the benefits in terms of business results.

CASE STUDY 6.2: MERLIN INTERNATIONAL

by Frank Cost, Rochester Institute of Technology

Merlin International is a small purely digital print provider in Rochester, New York. It grew out of an effort in 1995 when the RIT Research Corporation was approached by Nashua Corporation (*http://www.nashua.com*) with a request for a proposal to develop a system to automatically scan 35mm color negative film and produce digital color prints using a dry toner electrophotographic printing process. Nashua was at the time a major player in the conventional photofinishing market, as well as a manufacturer of toner for office printing applications. The idea was to develop a digital replacement for chemical photofinishing that would eventually enable Nashua to expand its toner business into an entirely new application domain.

The development effort was led by Gaurav Govil at RIT Research Corporation, and William Langille at Nashua Corporation. The project involved the integration of two of the most advanced devices for film scanning and digital color printing that existed at the time. The printing press selected was the first-generation Xeikon 32D digital color press, one of the leading-edge technologies in the mid-1990s. Merlin International was formed when RIT and Nashua created a separate business to pursue the development efforts.

Shortly after development work on the system began, the Merlin engineering team began to uncover the shortcomings of the selected technologies. The two most serious shortcomings were lower than expected image quality for the given application, and higher than expected consumable costs. Nashua withdrew from the development effort after it was determined that the technology would not be able to deliver the required end product.

In 1996, the development team headed by Douglas Smith decided to purchase the material assets from Nashua. Douglas Smith and the other Merlin owners had had many years of collective experience as developers of electrophotographic printing systems in their previous careers. Smith himself had recently retired from a long and distinguished career at Eastman Kodak Company. They therefore understood well how the Xeikon engine worked, and how it could be optimized to produce the highest quality color output. They were also able to service the machine themselves, avoiding the need to rely on service from Xeikon to keep the machine running. This gave Merlin a distinct advantage over other early entrants into the digital color printing market. Merlin was able to get the highest possible quality output from the

Xeikon engine at the lowest possible cost. Their early experimentation with coatings and laminates while conducting developmental work for Nashua also differentiated them from early commercial competitors.

Merlin's marketing strategy focused on clients who were seeking to build new commercial applications for digital color printing. The fledgling company was able to secure contracts with companies like Deluxe Corporation, a leading check and business forms printer that was seeking to diversify its service offerings by leveraging the new capabilities of digital printing to enable demand production of business communication products. The work gradually gave way to increasing production of short-run color print products such as brochures, manuals, and sell sheets for local commercial clients.

The commercial business grew largely by word of mouth during the years 1996 through 2000. Through these years, the company acquired five additional Xeikon engines, including the 50D machine that enabled continuous printing on rolls up to 50 centimeters (19.5 inches) wide. This enabled Merlin to produce a wider range of products, including signs for the retail point-of-purchase market. The company moved twice during this period as it added printing and finishing capacity. On the eve of the business recession that began in 2000, the company was doing more than three million dollars worth of business annually and had just moved into its current facility on Brooks Avenue in Chili, a suburb of Rochester.

The company suffered from a sharp reduction in business during the recession. Fortunately the owners had not amassed an unserviceable debt during their years of expansion. They had purchased used equipment and relied on their engineering talents to improve the performance to meet the quality expectations of their customers. They benefited in one important way from the general failure of digital color printing markets to grow rapidly in the last half of the 1990s. Many larger companies had made significant investments in digital printers and supporting infrastructure only to find that the anticipated markets for these services did not materialize as they had expected. Merlin was able to acquire equipment on excellent terms, keeping their fixed costs low enough to weather the recession and remain in business.

Today Merlin serves a growing number of customers with a variety of services that range from traditional short-run commercial printing to complex variable data printing and fulfillment services that integrate tightly with their customers' business processes. The average number of jobs in the plant on any given day ranges from 30–50, with nearly half of the work involving some kind of variable content. Because the company stayed with Xeikon print engines, they are also able to serve customers who need products that can only be produced on roll-fed machines that can print continuous images. These include wide format signage and decorative products.

The company still relies largely on repeat business and referrals from existing customers for new business. Merlin has only one full-time salesperson, and does not pursue an aggressive growth policy. Instead, the company concentrates on delivering high quality products and excellent service to its existing customers and trusts that new business opportunities will emerge as its reputation spreads. This conservative approach may not be the kind of business in which investors take much interest. But it has enabled one of the first companies to enter the digital color printing arena more than a decade ago to survive a tumultuous decade that defeated most other contenders, both large and small.

ENDNOTES FOR CHAPTER 6

94. Pellow, Pletka, and Banis, *Investing in Digital Color...The Bottom Line* (PICRM-2003-10).
95. Sorce and Pletka, *Digital Printing Success Models: Validation Study* (PICRM-2004-06).
96. All figures and tables in this chapter are from Sorce and Pletka, *Digital Printing Success Models: Validation Study* (PICRM-2004-06) unless otherwise indicated.
97. In the survey questionnaires, we used the term "variable data printing" to describe the range of data-driven print options available to create customized documents. This term was commonly used by the printing industry to describe the digital printing technology that allowed for unique content to be printed on each page. We will use VDP throughout this chapter in accordance with the precise wording used in the research program.
98. The 5% trimmed mean is reported because it removes the upper and lower 2.5% of the data points and then computes the mean of the remaining data. This does not imply that all outliers have been removed in the trimmed mean, but only the most extreme.
99. Pellow, Pletka, and Banis, *Investing in Digital Color...The Bottom Line* (PICRM-2003-10).
100. Pellow,"Bills Can Bring More than Just Headaches."

CHAPTER SEVEN

CREATING THE RIGHT BUSINESS STRATEGY AND SYSTEM FOR SELLING DATA-DRIVEN PRINT

WHEN THE FIRST DIGITAL COLOR PRESSES came out in the mid-1990s, a few entrepreneurs immediately saw the opportunity for personalized print communications and bought digital equipment. However, within five years, many of these innovators were either no longer in business, acquired by other firms, or missing the original digital equipment because they had decided to remove it![101] These disappointing business results were caused in part by the unreliability of the early digital presses, but the lack of business acumen of early adopters was also a factor.

RIT researchers sought out the early adopters, and discovered that firms that were no longer in business had three things in common:

1. no existing customer base that had an immediate need for these communications,
2. an imprecise growth strategy to attract new customers, and
3. little appreciation for the need to educate new customers about the benefits of customized print communications.

When asked why they had invested in digital printing equipment in the first place, a majority (61%) of all the innovators, both successful and unsuccessful, reported that it was because of "managerial instinct." They apparently had a sense that this should be a good market opportunity, but it often was unrealized because they lacked a sound growth strategy to capitalize on the opportunity.

The purpose of this chapter is to define the type of relevant growth strategy a firm will need to expand into data-driven print, and the requisite management systems that are also needed to deliver it. A growth strategy specifies what markets the firm will target with products and services that deliver a precise set of benefits. Once the strategy is in place, the resources of the firm must be organized to implement the strategy. Three crucial management systems must also be in place to manage these resources: operations, human resources, and sales management.

GROWTH STRATEGIES

A sound business plan includes a clearly-defined growth strategy. There are only two ways for a business to grow by offering a new product or service: either sell the new product or service to existing customers, or find new customers. The former is called *product development strategy*—the business grows by gaining new capabilities and then selling new products and services to existing customers.[102]

Successful digital color printing businesses have had a varied history of growth and development using this strategy. Many firms that originally started as commercial print providers or copy shops added digital color printing capabilities to serve their client's needs for print-on-demand or short-run color printing.[103] Some advertising and direct marketing agencies that previously outsourced their printing needs to commercial printers now offer the services themselves since they could not find reliable commercial printers who had that capability. Because the new digital color printing technology is capable of "clean" printing (minus the inks, fountain solutions, blanket wash, and volatile organic compounds that proliferate in an offset environment), these agencies can add digital production presses right in-house to assist clients who are expanding their marketing programs and want to take advantage of customer relationship management (CRM) systems.

With a product development strategy, a print services provider must be able to accurately forecast whether an investment in new digital print technology will enable the provider to leverage its existing customer base to sell data-driven print. The key is to carefully assess the marketing communications needs of the existing client base. Does the print services client have customers for whom a customized communication program makes sense? And does the client have the resources, both in terms of dollars and data, to carry it out? Perhaps a client that manufactures high-cost capital goods sold through its own sales force would benefit from up-to-date sales collateral customized to each customer. Or, a small business with local customers might increase profits by using targeted communications such as direct mail customized by geographic area.

The second growth approach is called *diversification*. Using this approach, a business cultivates new capabilities to appeal to a new set of customers.[104] Start-up businesses do just that—they develop new services for new customers. Many printing firms with digital printing capabilities have used a diversification strategy by targeting new business clients who have good internal data on their own customers. Industries such as financial services/insurance firms, manufacturing firms, and retail firms have a long history of gathering data about customers and using computers to facilitate billing and buying transactions. Nearly half of the digital print services firms we surveyed for our business model study (Chapter 6) had targeted these specific industries to sell their digital printing services.[105]

Offering new capabilities to find new customers, the diversification strategy can also be accomplished through an *integrative growth strategy*. Instead of developing a new capability internally, a firm might work with a supplier or a distributor to offer new capabilities.[106] For example, a print services provider that buys a mailing and fulfillment operation from a supplier is applying *vertical integration*. On the other hand, a firm that actually acquires a competitor with unique capabilities is taking advantage of *horizontal integration*. For example, an offset print provider may acquire a digital print provider or vice versa, as in the case of the RR Donnelley and Moore Wallace merger. In horizontal integration, the buying firm acquires the capabilities not by developing them internally but by purchasing the proven capability and clients of another.

Once the growth strategy is established, as we saw in Chapter 4, firms must next articulate a clearly-defined value discipline. Treacy and Wiersema identified three,[107] two of which allow businesses to charge a higher price for their products and services because they deliver a superior value. These two are *product leadership*, built upon superior product innovation, and *customer intimacy*, built on superior customer knowledge and service. The third strategy—*operational excellence*, built on superior internal operations—allows businesses to profit from being price leaders because of efficient production and distribution systems.

Companies can be successful with any of these three strategies. What is required, though, is *having* one. That is, strategic clarity in top management is the hallmark of successful firms. Using data from PIA/GATF's 2002 *Strategic Operating Assessment*, Printing Industry Center researchers Freeman and Rothenberg found that top printing firms (profit leaders) had a strategy of either "specialized low-cost" or "high value-added."[108] In contrast, profit laggards said they used a "general commercial printer" strategy. Table 7.1 compares the self-identified strategies between these profit leaders and laggards.

Table 7.1 *Print services providers' strategy options*[109]

	GENERAL COMMERCIAL PRINTER	SPECIALIZED LOW-COST PRINTER	SPECIALIZED HIGH VALUE-ADDED	OTHER
PROFIT LEADERS	63%	10%	22%	5%
PROFIT LAGGARDS	72%	5%	16%	11%

Once the strategy has been formalized in the business plan, a firm must implement it. The appropriate management systems for both human and technological resources must be in place or be developed to deliver the capabilities that the strategy calls for. For human resources, staffing, training, and motivation are key considerations. For the technological resources, besides having the adequate printing production technology, efficient operations are critical to ensure the quality and timeliness of printed products. In the next section we refer to another Printing Industry Center study that identifies the types of internal management systems that printing companies need in order to achieve revenue growth through product development or diversification.

MANAGEMENT SYSTEMS

Operations Management

For many industries, technology advances have resulted in an oversupply of goods and services that put extreme pressure on prices. This is especially true for traditional manufacturing processes that characterize much of print production in the U.S. As reported in the 2004 PIA/GATF Ratios survey, the profit leaders in the printing industry are simply more efficient at manufacturing the printed product.[110]

While new technology can reduce the costs of business and manufacturing processes, its acquisition in the absence of a disciplined approach to process analysis and improvement can sometimes lead in the wrong direction—to increased costs and eventual failure. In order to survive, many print services providers have had to re-engineer their production processes to include the latest efficient manufacturing techniques. This *lean manufacturing* approach is made up of two important elements:

1. performance metrics with root cause analysis to determine the causes of unnecessary steps in the production process, and
2. information integration across the production workflow.

In a survey of manufacturing practices conducted by the Printing Industry Center at RIT, Cost and Daly found that while lean manufacturing practices are recognized as important, there is a gap between knowledge and standard practice.[111] Almost all the firms surveyed used performance metrics to assess on-time delivery, but a substantial percentage of respondents "never" measured ink waste (48%) or paper waste (15%). While the majority of firms reported that their production employees had some quality control training (74%), only half said that this included statistical process control and root cause analysis, which are at the heart of lean production control processes, and the hallmark of six-sigma programs.

The second element of lean manufacturing is getting pertinent information about production processes to top management and anyone who needs it on the production floor. Over half of the survey respondents reported that they had management information systems in place, but fewer than half used them to schedule or plan production. Larger firms were more likely to have and use systems such as enterprise resource planning (ERP). And while monitoring and controlling the production process is crucial for lowering costs on a continuous basis, less than half of the firms (44%) said that they had cost reduction goals for the coming year. Clearly, there is a gap between knowing what needs to be done to improve operational efficiency and actually doing it.

An excellent operations management system can deliver a competitive advantage because many print providers don't yet have these systems in place. Although smaller companies may be less likely to take a comprehensive approach to manufacturing cost reduction, they still stand to benefit from a working knowledge of how lean manufacturing practices and computer integration can be put to work in a print-manufacturing context.

Human Resource Management

Actually delivering the new products and services that technology has made possible often requires new skills for the workforce. Because new computer-integrated production systems demand these high-level skills on the part of employees, human resource management itself has become a key function to ensure good recruiting, training, retaining, and compensating practices.

An important workforce capability for many digital print services providers is information technology (IT). As we saw in Chapter 6, firms that specialize in Internet on-demand or full service/fully customized printed programs have hired larger IT staffs than those based on a quick print model. IT know-how allows a firm to provide additional services to its clients, such as database and list management. Print services providers that produced complex variable data printing applications were also more likely to offer additional IT services.[112] Table 7.2 verifies this.

Table 7.2 *Percent of digital printers offering additional services*[113]

SERVICE	OVERALL	QUICK PRINT	SHORT RUN	IOD	FS/FC
DATABASE MANAGEMENT	72%	57%	68%	73%	84%
DATA MINING	33%	15%	13%	42%	51%
LIST MANAGEMENT	47%	30%	45%	58%	55%
EMAIL MARKETING	32%	21%	10%	38%	48%

While some firms hire new employees with IT skills, training current employees for new job functions is also a viable option. In fact, the 2004 PIA/GATF study of leading printing firms found that training programs are highly correlated with profitability.[114] Freeman and Rothenberg agree: profit leaders invested the equivalent of over 3% of their payroll in training and education while profit laggards only invested about 1% in training (see Table 7.3).

Table 7.3 *Training practices of profit leaders and laggards*[115]

PERCENT OF PAYROLL COSTS DEVOTED TO TRAINING AND EDUCATION	
PROFIT LEADERS	3.29%
PROFIT LAGGARDS	1.34%

These training practices are not just for production employees. As shown in Table 7.4, profit leaders are also more likely to provide training programs for top management, administrators, and customer service and sales employees.

Table 7.4 *Training practices of profit leaders and laggards by position*[116]

	TOP MANAGEMENT*	ADMINISTRATORS*	SALES/ CUSTOMER SERVICE*
PROFIT LEADERS	14%	10%	39%
PROFIT LAGGARDS	2%	0%	21%

**T-Test shows a significant difference in means. Results are significant to the .05 level.*

The third important human resource policy is adequate compensation. Many successful firms share their profits with the people who helped attain them. Freeman and Rothenberg found that employee participation in profits through ownership, profit-sharing plans, or bonus systems significantly differentiated the profit leaders and laggards. More than 60% of profit leaders offered some participation to all employees, versus only 40% of laggards. The human resources department of a firm needs to find the right people with the right skills, and nurture and reward them with training programs and profit-sharing compensations policies. Without motivated employees, any business will certainly fail.

Sales Management

While strategic planning is ultimately the responsibility of top management, it often falls to the sales force to actually execute a growth strategy. Given the task of selling data-driven print, the successful sales force will emphasize efficiency as the primary benefit to the client. Rather than communicating to a large undifferentiated audience, data-driven print materials will allow the client to print and distribute fewer pieces to a precisely defined target and still achieve the revenue goals of the campaign. The sales representative is making the claim that the client can print less and sell more. This new sales paradigm is a challenge for experienced printing sales representatives, because they have to change the way they go about selling to clients. Success in promoting data-driven communications usually only happens when the contact with a potential client is at the marketing decision level, such as interactions with a VP of marketing rather than with the procurement manager or print buyer.

More than half of the owners and managers of successful digital printing firms in a 2003 RIT study felt that their sales force had average to very little expertise in selling variable data printing services.[117] Why is this? Offset printing sales representatives have traditionally promoted the benefits of high print volumes: the larger the quantity printed, the lower the unit cost. Since sales commissions are often based on simple revenue, it has been in the best interest of sales reps to maximize the volume of print that is ordered, even if this was not the optimal solution for the client. But now, the key to selling data-driven printing is to assist clients in developing "smarter" marketing programs that likely use fewer printed pieces. The data-driven print sales representative must convince a client that buying and mailing fewer printed pieces, correctly customized to the needs of prospective customers, will deliver a better sales response than mailing a larger quantity that is not customized. This scenario will only work if the sales representative helps his or her client to create higher-value communications. (See Appendix 7.1: *Selling Small and Smart.*)

Actually, data-driven print sales representatives are selling a program rather than a printed commodity. Salespeople will be successful selling data-driven print if they help clients plan campaigns where customized marketing communications make sense. This isn't easy. When asked what challenges digital print providers face in selling variable data printing, nearly all of the respondents to one of our recent surveys (84.1%) reported the need to communicate the value of personalization to their clients.[118] Clients often do not have a retention or customer relationship strategy that would make them ask for the efficiencies delivered by customized marketing communication programs.

The successful data-driven print provider may also need to offer additional services to leverage the information resources that a client firm will need to build to make custom marketing possible. While these IT resources may initially be very costly to develop, after the print provider and the client have invested a significant amount of time and resources in them, the client will tend to keep doing business with the salesperson's firm because of high switching costs. If the print provider keeps a client's digital assets and data stored at the printing facility, reordering jobs will be simple, especially if the print provider has a Web-based ordering interface. Reordering can then be as easy as a click of the mouse. When a targeted application is designed and executed successfully, clients will tend to request smaller orders more frequently. The timeliness and convenience of this process will be perceived as an additional benefit of doing business with the print services provider, and at the same time will allow the print provider to charge a higher price. Overall, this is an ideal setting for selling digital printing, and those who have attempted it thus far have been very successful. See the case study on Lexinet at the end of the chapter (Case Study 7.1, p. 122).

In sum, the sales team that succeeds at selling data-driven print is the one that has demonstrated the value of executing smaller, smarter marketing campaigns. In order to do this, the impact of a campaign must be calculated, so the selling cycle will not end with the mailing of the printed pieces. In the next chapter, we will see how the successful data-driven print provider closes the loop on the communications process.

CONCLUSION

The early adopters of digital printing technologies have shown us, despite their own failures, how to build a profitable business. A successful print provider must have a sound business strategy that matches its capabilities to a known set of customer needs, as well as the implementation skills and sound management practices that can deliver the new capabilities of data-driven print communications. Technology alone cannot deliver good business results. The sales force also must understand its role in the process—to help clients meet their marketing goals. While the business model of a successful data-driven print services provider is complex, it can deliver many benefits if the provider is willing to optimize its technical and human resources to serve the needs of its clients.

APPENDIX 7.1:
SELLING SMALL AND SMART

by Sandra Rothenberg, Rochester Institute of Technology

As society faces environmental limits to material consumption, the typical business model's goal of "selling large" must be questioned. In the seminal book *Small is Beautiful*,[119] Schumacher argues that in order to be a truly sustainable society, we must ultimately consume less. The Printing Industry Center at RIT research report *Selling Small and Smart: The Future of the Sustainable Enterprise* (PICRM-2004-01)[120] outlines the experiences of three suppliers that are operating under a new business model that allows economic growth, while also helping society to step away from the spiral of increasing consumption.

In this new business model, material goods are not seen as ends in themselves. The traditional model of selling as much as possible is abandoned in exchange for a model in which firms make money by helping their customers achieve their goals while using less product.

THREE CASES

The experiences of three companies, PPG (a paint supplier), Gage Chemical, and Xerox, show how the switch to a sustainable business model can be successful. (See Table 7.5.) In addition to the reduction of product use, other environmental benefits were seen in all three cases.

Table 7.5 *Summary of three cases of "Selling Small"*

	GAGE	PPG	XEROX
OLD MODEL OF "SELLING LARGE"	Selling chemical blends for automotive paint application	Selling paint for automotive paint application	Selling printers, copiers, and supporting products
NEW "SELLING SMALL" MODEL	Providing an effective paint shop operation	Managing efficient and quality paint shop operations	Managing efficient document management processes
MATERIAL GOODS REDUCED	Solvents and cleaners	Paint	Printers, copiers, paper, and toner
OTHER ENVIRONMENTAL BENEFITS	Lower VOC emissions	Lower VOC emissions	Less energy use and reduced solid waste

BRINGING ABOUT A CULTURAL SHIFT

The move to selling small is not easy. This new business model challenges one of the most basic assumptions about the goal of the average manufacturing organization, namely, that selling more of a product is good for the organization, and selling less of a product is bad. Internally, this basic assumption about the very nature of the firm is likely to be challenged, requiring attention to cultural change. Firms need to reframe the usual operating assumption from, "The goal of our firm is to sell more product," to, "The goal of our firm is to help our customers do X, and use less of our product in the process."

A Xerox spokesman explained the conflict: "It is a tough [transition] because you are now selling an intangible alongside the tangible, and the intangible (the services and optimization) is often the more important component of the transaction. ... [But] when you ultimately concentrate on what is right for the client, the client is inherently going to give you more business and more revenue, which is an offset to the declining product element of a transaction."

Bringing about a cultural shift in employees' minds is not the only challenge to firms that are trying to "sell small and smart." They also need to change sales incentive structures and the skill base within their organizations. Also, at the operational level of the customer organization, reductions in the use of various materials are likely to mean changing long-held routines and assumptions.

HOW TO MAKE THE SWITCH

Given these challenges, how can firms manage the change to selling small? Drawing from the experiences of PPG, Gage, and Xerox, there are some general steps that can be followed for firms wanting to make the shift to selling small:

- **Build off existing strengths:** Often, suppliers are in the best position to help their customers use less of their product. Recognize and build off existing technical expertise about the product and the customer operation in which it is used. In the experience of Gage Chemical and PPG, for example, there was already a service mindset that helped employees understand the new role they were playing for their customers. Xerox, on the other hand, built off an existing base of technical expertise, which contributed to the detailed process information needed to help customers find ways to use less product.

- **Redefine the basis for profit in contractual agreements:** Traditional contracts, usually based on compensation per unit sold, rarely offer any incentive for suppliers to help consumers use less of their product. New contracts need to offer "win-win" alternatives, in which both parties can benefit from reduced sales of the traditional product. These contracts can even include explicit goals for product use reduction and associated environmental goals. Gage, for example, changed the way it sold its material from a per gallon basis to a "cost per unit" basis, where the customer paid a set amount per vehicle being painted. Using a slightly different approach, PPG and Chrysler reformulated their traditional contracts so that both parties shared cost reductions achieved by supplier initiatives.

- **Communicate the new business model:** Selling small does not fit into the traditional business model, but rather it challenges basic assumptions and requires change for both the supplier and customer. Leaders need to continuously communicate, to all parties involved, the value of reducing product use and sales.

- **Change incentives:** Most firms working under the "selling large" model offer incentives tied to increased product sales. These incentive systems need to change to allow salespeople and other employees make the connection between selling small and their own personal compensation. Gage, for example, eliminated commissions. Xerox has stopped paying some employees on a transaction-by-transaction basis. Instead, they are paid according to the year-over-year revenue increase from their customer base or their targeted geography.

- **Acquire new employee skills and knowledge:** While suppliers need to build off their existing skills and knowledge, it is likely that these are not sufficient to fully implement the new business model. Additional customer service skills or technical knowledge about customer processes may be needed. For some companies, acquiring the appropriate skills may only involve retraining workers. All three firms we interviewed adjusted their service training to meet the needs of their new business models. For others, it may involve hiring workers with specialized knowledge about customer processes or even acquiring another firm. Xerox, for example, purchased an entire company in order to obtain an expertise in information technology.

- **Highlight environmental advantages:** Most approaches to selling small are motivated by customer interest in reducing cost. Yet the environmental benefits are also real and sometimes significant. Some suppliers will be approached by customers already interested in reducing environmental impact. For those that aren't, the environmental benefits of reduced product use can be a strong component of the marketing effort.

Firms are likely to be more successful selling small if there is pressure for change, coming either from the customers, as in the case of PPG and Gage, or from the market, as in the case of Xerox. The key to sustaining a selling small strategy is building close relationships with customers, in which they come to depend on the supplier for their process knowledge. Thus, firms that want to sell small require an in-depth knowledge of their customers' processes and needs, as well as close service relationships with them. Sometimes the selling small approach itself can build a closer relationship with a customer, increasing revenues in the process. In addition, because they are better able to propose innovative process solutions, firms with a broad product base and strong R&D department will benefit more from selling small than those suppliers who only produce one particular product.

The motivation to use less product is usually primarily economic. But, as Xerox found, proactive and environmentally aware customers also recognize the environmental benefits of reducing material use. Suppliers can educate their customers about the synergies between environmental performance and cost reduction. Framing services as a means to help both the environmental and financial bottom line makes an attractive proposition for customers.

As pressures for reduced material consumption become more salient, it is likely that this new model will become more common. The question for most manufacturers of products is not whether they should move to selling small, but when. As in other areas of service provision, early movers will have the advantage.

CASE STUDY 7.1: LEXINET[121]

Lexinet began operations in 1991 when Dan Adler and Lisa Boyer, consultants who had perfected multiple-dealer mailing programs, decided it was time to join forces. Based on their direct-marketing backgrounds and understanding of technology, they had a clear vision for a company. They wanted to deliver on-demand direct mail programs that were personalized, and localized ones that were organized and managed through the Internet.

BUILDING THE INFRASTRUCTURE

The driving force behind Lexinet's success was the development of a software support infrastructure that enabled clients to efficiently and effectively deliver relevant messages to customers. Also critical was allowing companies to compose their own mailings from a variety of existing templates written to customer specifications. Lexinet enables its customers to create mailings with unlimited high resolution variables—both text and images—to customize and personalize direct-mail messages. Lexinet maintains a workflow that seamlessly integrates with its customers' organizations, ensuring that customers are able to initiate mail campaigns twenty-four hours a day, seven days a week.

The first step in the evolution of the business was software development. Lexinet developed proprietary software for a multi-option, multi-variable, multi-location mailing system. This software was Lexinet's differentiated value-added service for building a profitable business. According to Adler, "No investment was made in print technology until the software was complete and we had an identified customer base that would generate ample revenue to make the monthly payments on printing equipment." The company's first laser printing technology, a Xerox 4650, was used to produce customized mailers that combined offset printed shells with personalized messaging.

Alder kept close tabs on developments in printing technology, and saw an opportunity with the Xerox DocuTech. Adler stated, "The ability to integrate high quality photo images into direct mailers for key target markets including insurance and real estate offered significant new business potential. DocuTech's ability to print on 11 x 17 paper opened up the market opportunity for custom newsletters. In addition, the migration to industry standard workflows made the transition to digital color much easier." Today, Lexinet has two Xerox iGens, a DocuColor 12, and the Xerox Nuvera in its equipment fleet.

THE RESOURCES: DATA AND PEOPLE

According to Adler and Boyer, "It all starts with the data. The biggest challenge clients have is developing a simple mechanism for leveraging data for targeted mailings." While Lexinet offers a full portfolio of digital services, its customers place the highest level of value on the company's ability to manage and manipulate database information. Lexinet has developed several unique systems to handle all kinds of files, from some of the most sophisticated relational database files provided by large data centers to the more common basic formats generated by users from their desktop PCs.

Lexinet also maintains a complete database of all U.S. households through a license agreement with a national compiler. With advanced data-processing capability, the company is able to blend these lists with clients' customer and prospect lists. This means that users have quick access to an extensive database for targeted promotions.

Lexinet can import or export information to and from any platform, from mainframe to PC to diskettes and CDs, as well as facilitate and utilize online file transfers. File enhancements and data hygiene capabilities include PAVE/CASS Certified Postal Software, address standardization, NCOA, gender coding, and name splitting. The company handles all the most common printer languages, including PostScript, PCL, TIFF, PDF and ASCII text. If a client requires data entry of raw typed or hand-written addresses, that service is also provided.

This state-of-the-art data processing and warehousing capability is combined with custom programming; creative service support; digital printing, mailing and fulfillment; and detailed analysis of campaign effectiveness to round out Lexinet's unique portfolio.

Implementation of these data-driven programs required significant technical resources. Lexinet has five full-time people dedicated to database administration, Web programming and creative services. When asked how Lexinet recovers costs associated with staffing resources, Boyer said, "Our customers understand the value we bring. Every program is different, but the marketing executive knows that programming isn't free. We have established a setup fee for getting the program up and running. This will vary with the complexity of the program. There is a monthly fee for hosting the site and customer support. Finally, there is a base package charge for mailing each piece."

THE SALES STRATEGY

With their direct mail backgrounds, Adler and Boyer realized that selling direct mail programs was a complex endeavor. Rather than building a large direct sales force, their focus has been on educating creative agencies about how new technology can re-engineer direct mail campaigns. They share with agencies the benefits of both a dealerized, personalized approach, and the unique hardware and software technology Lexinet has to support implementation. Lexinet consults with advertising agencies for direct mail campaigns. This is a sales strategy that has worked well for Lexinet, with 2002 revenues climbing 34%.

THE THRIVENT ACCOUNT

Lexinet provides a comprehensive direct mail program for Thrivent Financial for Lutherans' insurance agents. Thrivent wanted to provide its field sales force with an on-demand direct mail program to generate new sales or cross-sell different insurance programs. While this program would require flexibility, versatility, and timeliness, Thrivent also wanted to ensure that corporate headquarters could tightly control information being distributed to customers and potential customers. Lexinet set up an extensive menu of messages, formats, and data mining features from which Thrivent representatives could choose. Personal sales representative information could be incorporated into each mailing piece, including photos, scanned signatures, and titles. Because sales reps had varying levels of access to technology, Lexinet offered multiple channels through which to place orders—phone, fax, mail, or Internet—and provided three-to-five-day turnaround times for direct mail requests. Thrivent also wanted its field reps to communicate with the corporate marketing department on all field activity in order to generate an ongoing analysis of the business results.

The Thrivent application is one of many dealer/agent solutions that Lexinet provides to clients by leveraging a full document services portfolio and the company's digital printing technology. According to Boyer, "The critical success factor is putting the power of customized direct mail into the hands of the individual closest to the customer. Dealers, agents and franchisees are all looking for ways to differentiate their messages on a local level."

CONCLUSION

Lexinet is an excellent example of a company that took the right steps to build a digital business. The company chose a value proposition in which data was king: helping clients construct data, providing user access to the data, executing data programs, and analyzing results. Lexinet's business model took the following form:

- The business was started with a clear vision and a solid business plan. Solutions are personalized and customized, providing maximum control to the ultimate end user.
- The development of a database and a data-driven model encourages a strong long-term relationship with clients and enables Lexinet to predict print volume and resource requirements.
- Lexinet's model is full-service with value-added differentiation, from Internet user interfaces for order entry all the way to the distribution of customized printed material to the end customer.

ENDNOTES TO CHAPTER 7

101. Pellow, Frey, and Sorce, *Digital Color: Where Is the Market?* (PICRM-2002-02).
102. Kotler, *Marketing Management.*
103. Sorce and Pletka, *Digital Printing Success Models* (PICRM-2004-06).
104. Kotler, *Marketing Management.* Two other growth strategies also involve selling more existing products. One is "market penetration," in which a company sells more existing products, or more services, to existing customers. The other is "market development," in which a company sells existing products and services to new customers, often by expanding geographically.
105. Sorce and Pletka, *Digital Printing Success Models* (PICRM-2004-06).
106. Kotler, *Marketing Management.*
107. Treacy and Wiersema, *The Discipline of Market Leaders.*
108. Freeman and Rothenberg, *Success Under Adversity* (PICRM-2004-10).
109. Ibid.
110. Davis, "Printers, Payroll, and Profitability."
111. Cost and Daly, *Digital Integration and Lean Manufacturing Practices of U.S. Printing Firms* (PICRM-2003-09).
112. Sorce and Pletka, *Digital Printing Success Models* (PICRM-2004-06).
113. Ibid.
114. Davis, "Printers, Payroll, and Profitability."
115. Freeman and Rothenberg, *Success Under Adversity* (PICRM-2004-10).
116. Ibid.
117. Pellow and Sorce, *The Role of Value-Added Services in Successful Digital Printing* (PICRM-2003-02).
118. Sorce and Pletka, *Digital Printing Success Models* (PICRM-2004-06).
119. Schumacher, *Small is Beautiful.*
120. Rothenberg, *Selling Small and Smart* (PICRM-2004-01).

121. Pellow, Pletka, and Banis, *Investing in Digital Color...The Bottom Line* (PICRM-2003-10).

CHAPTER EIGHT

MEASURING SUCCESS: CLOSING THE FEEDBACK LOOP

THE CHALLENGE: The most complex types of customized marketing communications require meaningful knowledge of current customers, and capturing and using this knowledge involves a large investment of firm resources. In this marketing strategy, growing the value of customers over time is the primary objective. The quality of the data-driven communications is more important than the quantity of contacts sales representatives may make with customers. In order for a company to commit to the level of investment required for implementing customized marketing communications, top management must first understand the value of these programs. So we turn to measuring outcomes, that is, evaluating how these data-driven tactics compare to standard marketing communications regarding revenues and profits.

This chapter describes how marketers assess the effectiveness of the marketing function. Then we look at a metric that has received a lot of attention recently: lifetime value (LTV).

A MYRIAD OF METHODS

Measuring the effectiveness of a marketing program is a challenge that has been with business for decades. The PIMS (Profit Impact of Market Strategy) business information database, accessed at *www.pimsonline.com*, gives real world business performance experiences of more than 3,000 businesses, representing 16,000+ years of data.[122] A quick look at the wealth of this PIMS data will reinforce the fact that this measurement issue is not a simple one.

Assessing the impact of a marketing program can be carried out at the boardroom level (by asking, for example, whether marketing expenditures can be linked to overall financial measures such as shareholder value), or at the tactical level (again by asking, for example, which changes in a marketing promotion produced the revenue achieved). The measures assessed can be long-term in scope, like brand asset valuation, or short-term, like tabulating the number of coupons redeemed for a specific promotion. The measures can be tracked internally, for example by tracing the number of hits on a Web site, or outsourced to a firm such as a trade association that tracks total market size across all competitors in an industry in order to determine an individual firm's market size. The measures can be simple counts such as how many prospects return a reply card, or they can be the result of complex statistical modeling to predict sales volume as a function of marketing expenditures, competitive responses, and overall economic factors.

In general, most large corporations use more than one marketing metric.[123] In a study of over 700 of the leading advertisers in their industries, approximately four metrics were used per corporation in annual reports to respective corporate boards. The most frequently used metrics were:

- market share (79%),
- perceived product or service quality (77%),
- customer retention (64%), and
- customer profitability (64%).

A different survey of a small number of leading U.S. firms concluded that the most popular metrics of overall marketing performance at the strategic business unit (SBU) level were market share, sales, and profits.[124] The choice of metrics should be determined by the nature of the firm, the competitive strategy, and the particular marketing challenges the firm faces.[125]

Once a measure or set of measures have been determined, there remains an additional challenge: *predictive validity*. Can we associate the outcome measure (market share, revenue, or profits) to a change in the marketing strategy (for example, increased spending on advertising)? How can we separate the impact of an adjustment to advertising spending from other factors in the environment, such as improved economic conditions or a change in a competitor's marketing strategy? Complex econometric models have been designed to quantify the contributions of marketing mix factors on the financial performance of a firm.[126]

For marketers without statistical expertise or solid database resources, the ability to use complex modeling is limited. Many marketers use simpler metrics to assess the impact of specific marketing communication tactics on measurable outcomes within a limited time frame. For example, the impact of a local Superbowl promotion (*specific tactic*) can be calculated by noting the change in weekly sales (*outcome measure*) before and after the promotion has run (*time frame*). Common tools used to gauge the effectiveness of advertising and other promotional tactics are outlined in the following section.

ADVERTISING EFFECTIVENESS MEASURES: THE HIERARCHY OF EFFECTS

Accountability is the watchword for marketing and advertising managers in today's business environment.[127] This comes after years of relatively uninhibited expenditures on mass printed and broadcast advertising, where the effects of the advertising are difficult to link to specific purchasing behavior. Today a marketing manager will have a hard time demonstrating conclusively that investments made in marketing, specifically in advertising and promotion, have improved outcome measures such as revenues and market share. Though direct marketing has historically been a strong marketing tactic, strict accountability is now being asked of it and all other marketing efforts.

Assessing the impact of a specific element of the marketing mix (for example, a certain campaign, or a price or packaging change) has become easier with the widespread use of *point-of-sale* information tracking, which provides a good outcome measure for products that are low in price and purchased frequently. For more expensive items that are purchased infrequently, a sales measure taken at a particular time may not be accurate because a lot of road is covered between a buyer's first exposure to a particular advertising message and his or her eventual trip to the cash register. This is illustrated in Figure 8.1 using the advertising *hierarchy of effects* model: buying is the end-point of a marketing communications process that is designed to create awareness, establish a preference, and then motivate the customer to buy the advertised product or service.[128] Though the hierarchy of effects model has been disputed recently as a reliable method for measuring the effectiveness of advertising,[129] it still is a useful starting point when articulating the communication goal of advertising during the planning stages of a marketing campaign.[130]

Figure 8.1 *The advertising hierarchy of effects model*[131]

Well-designed promotional programs always identify the communication outcome in the planning stages of a campaign. These measures are determined not only by the communications objectives of the campaign, but also by the nature of the product and its current stage in its *product life cycle*. For new brands or products, awareness is a common communication objective. For existing brands or products with longer purchase cycles, changing consumers' preferences is the objective. For products that are purchased frequently, a change in sales may be the stated objective of the marketing campaign. Appendix 8.1 at the end of this chapter discusses common advertising effectiveness measures, organized by the communications outcomes they measure.

Although direct marketing is usually a major facet of the marketing communications program of many firms, it has for a number of years been set apart from mass media communications planning. But the integrated communications era is now upon us, and metrics developed by direct marketers can be used more broadly to determine the return on marketing communications investments in general. The next section will examine metrics that have been developed to assess the outcomes of direct marketing methods.

DIRECT ADVERTISING, ROI, AND LTV

Media planning starts with cost per thousand (CPM), which is the cost to reach 1,000 people measured by audience size (broadcast), circulation (magazines and newspapers), or households that received direct mail. While this is a good starting point to assess the efficiency of different media choices, direct marketing specialists have developed an extensive array of metrics to gauge not only the revenue but also the profitability of a campaign.[132] Response per thousand (RPM) is a simple computation that captures the response measure, often measured in terms of inquiries, visits, or orders, related to the total number of people contacted.

$$\text{Response per thousand (RPM)} = \frac{\text{Total response (e.g., number of orders)}}{\text{Quantity contacted/1000}}$$

The cost per response (CPR) is determined by dividing the cost of contacting the audience by the total number that responded.

$$\text{Cost per response (CPR)} = \text{CPM/RPM}$$

For example, how will the owner of a new Thai restaurant in a suburban neighborhood of a small city choose between advertising its grand opening on cable TV or by direct mail? The media plan presented by an advertising agency would likely compare the cost per thousand (CPM) of the two media choices for reaching the target market of local, ethnic food lovers who like to dine out (see Table 8.1). In the first option, let's say a cable TV campaign requires $25,000 for producing the ad and $75,000 for broadcasting it to the 500,000 cable TV household subscribers in the region. The ad would be repeated 30 times during the week prior to the restaurant's opening event, and it would be shown on the Food Network, the Weather Channel, and during local news programs. Because the total cost is $100,000 for contacting 500,000 households, the CPM for this option would be $200. That is, for every 1,000 potential customers contacted, the restaurant owner would pay $200.

Compare this to a direct mail campaign. The advertising agency could buy a mailing list of the 20,000 homes within five miles of the new restaurant. A single mailing would appear in residents' mailboxes the week before the restaurant opens. If printing and mailing costs are $20,000, the CPM will be $1,000, or, for every 1,000 potential customers that the mailing will reach, the restaurant owner pays $1,000.

Table 8.1 *Comparison of two media choices for a hypothetical advertising campaign*

	PRODUCTION COSTS	MEDIA COSTS	NUMBER REACHED	CALCULATION OF CPM	CPM
CABLE TV	$25,000	$75,000	500,000	$\frac{\$100,000}{500,000/1000}$	$200
DIRECT MAIL	$10,000	$10,000	20,000	$\frac{\$20,000}{20,000/1000}$	$1,000

Which medium would you choose? If CPM is the most important consideration, you would obviously choose the cable TV ad because it delivers a lower CPM. Most mass media advertising will net a lower CPM than direct mailing methods. But a sophisticated media buyer is also concerned about the effectiveness of the advertising medium. A one-week, 30-slot exposure to 500,000 cable TV households will include a lot of wasted coverage. People who live 50 miles away from the restaurant may get the message, but won't be likely to drive that far to the grand opening. Perhaps if some work nearby, they may consider going for lunch. But how many people would even notice the cable TV ad? With a direct mail campaign, on the other hand, patrons can be targeted by geographic location. However, would a single mailing be enough to get the word out or to initiate action?

In order to effectively compare media choices, a marketer needs to measure the outcomes of communication efforts. Taking our example one step further, let's imagine what happens at the weekend grand opening event. Table 8.2 gives the response per thousand (RPM) and cost per response (CPR) for an outcome of 100 dinner patrons as the result of each media campaign.

Table 8.2 *RPM and CPR for an outcome of 100 dinner patrons*

	CPM (COST PER M)	NUMBER OF PATRONS (SALES RESPONSE)	RPM (RESPONSE PER M)	CPR (COST PER RESPONSE) (CPM/RPM)
CABLE TV	\$200	100	$\frac{100}{500{,}000/1000} = 0.2$	$\frac{\$200}{0.2} = \$1{,}000$
DIRECT MAIL	\$1,000	100	$\frac{100}{20{,}000/1000} = 5$	$\frac{\$1{,}000}{5} = \$200$

Using the RPM metric, the direct mail campaign appears to be more efficient, since the owner would generate five orders per thousand people contacted using direct mail, versus generating only .2 orders per thousand people contacted with cable TV. But the CPR metric gives the best reason to favor direct mail. The restaurant will only have to spend \$200 per order received with direct mail, versus spending \$1,000 to get one order from the cable TV campaign.

While these metrics are handy measures that can deliver the accountability that business decisions require, they often only measure the effectiveness of a single campaign on a short-term outcome, as in the example above. To track buying behavior over time, the measure of *lifetime value* (LTV) has been adopted. LTV is defined as "the net present value of the profit that you will realize on the average new customer during a given number of years."[133] Championed by loyalty marketing consultants, LTV computations provide a metric to assess whether an initial investment in acquiring new customers will pay off in the long run. Marketers can also use LTV as a framework for comparing the value of the customized printed communications used in direct mail advertising to the more common static or generic printed mailers.

For example, a fictional apparel catalog retailer called Great Northern wants to develop a new line of products that includes sports items such as golf, tennis, and skiing equipment, and target the new products to existing apparel customers. One approach to advertising this new line would be to develop a single catalog containing all of Great Northern's new sports equipment products, and then mail it to the company's list of apparel customers. The catalog would have static content and only the name and address of the customer would be printed on the cover for U.S. mail distribution. Let's say Great Northern sends such a common catalog to one million of their customers. In order to get an LTV computation for customers who respond during the first year, the revenues associated with each customer and the campaign costs must be calculated. Let's say Great Northern gives us the following data:

Table 8.3 *Hypothetical results from static/mail merge catalog campaign*

Response rate to new generic catalog (percent of catalog recipients who placed an order)	2%
Average number of new orders per year per customer	1.8
Size of order (average)	$450.00
Cost of goods sold, as a percentage of list price	70%
Cost of designing, printing and mailing the catalogs, per piece	$0.80
Discount rate (net present value, or NPV) - the discounted value of money.	0.12

Using traditional direct marketing metrics, if the mailing goes to one million households and 20,000 customers place an order, the CPR (cost per response) is $40.00 ($800,000 to mail the catalogs / 20,000 responses) and the RPM (number of orders per thousand catalogs mailed) is 36 (2% x 1,000 x 1.8). Table 8.4 calculates the LTV of these 20,000 customers who ordered from the new catalog, using the above assumptions and applying NPV (net present value) in the first year. (Some argue that NPV should first be applied in the second year).

Table 8.4 *LTV calculation for hypothetical static/mail merge catalog campaign*

	YEAR 1
CUSTOMER DATA	
# of mailings	1,000,000
Response rate	2.0%
# of customers acquired	20,000
# orders/year (average)	1.8
REVENUE DATA	
Average order size	$450
Total revenue per year	$16,200,000
Cost of goods sold (70% of list price)	$11,340,000
Net revenue	$4,860,000
MARKETING COSTS	
Cost per catalog (design, printing and postage)	$0.80
Total marketing cost	$800,000
PROFIT	
Net profit	$4,060,000
Discount rate	1.12
NPV profit	$3,625,000
AVERAGE CUSTOMER LTV (NPV PROFIT DIVIDED BY THE NUMBER OF CUSTOMERS ACQUIRED IN FIRST YEAR)	$181.25

This single promotion yields a NPV profit of $3.6 million in the first year. The LTV, though not a particularly useful metric in the first year, is $181.25 per customer acquired. The LTV metric becomes useful when we extend the timeframe to answer the question: What is the value of this customer base over time? If we assume that 60% of these customers who bought equipment in the first year buy again but gradually reduce the number of purchases they make over the next few years due to saturation or lifestyle changes, then we can calculate a four-year LTV. See Table 8.5.

Table 8.5 *Four-year LTV calculation for hypothetical static/mail merge catalog campaign*

	YEAR 1	YEAR 2	YEAR 3	YEAR 4
CUSTOMER DATA				
Retention rate		60%	60%	60%
# of customers	20,000	12,000	7,200	4,320
# orders/year	1.8	1.5	1.2	1
REVENUE DATA				
Average order	$450	$450	$450	$450
Total revenue	$16,200,000	$8,100,000	$3,888,000	$1,944,000
Cost of goods sold (70%)	$11,340,000	$5,670,000	$2,721,600	$1,360,800
Net revenue	$4,860,000	$2,430,000	$1,166,400	$583,200
MARKETING COSTS				
Cost per mailing	$0.80	$0.80	$0.80	$0.80
Total marketing cost (based on mailing to prior year's customers)	$800,000	$16,000	$9,600	$5,760
PROFIT				
Net profit	$4,060,000	$2,414,000	$1,156,800	$577,440
Discount rate	1.12	1.25	1.40	1.57
NPV profit	$3,625,000	$1,924,426	$823,387	$366,974
Cumulative NPV profit	$3,625,000	$5,549,426	$6,372,813	$6,739,787
AVG. CUSTOMER LTV	**$181.25**	**$277.47**	**$318.64**	**$336.99**
(on 20,000 customers acquired in year 1)		($5,549,426 /20,000)		

The LTV per customer recruited in the first year has grown, by the fourth year, to $337. This information alone is not particularly useful but sets a benchmark against the measure of "what-if" scenarios for different campaigns.

Now let's compare this static mailing with a customized catalog. Great Northern can customize its catalog based on the apparel purchasing behavior of its customers. For example, customers who purchased ski parkas can receive a ski equipment catalog, and those who purchased golf polos can receive a golf equipment catalog. We'll increase the hypothetical response rate in Table 8.6 to 5% because of the usual increased response rate to personalized campaigns, and we'll increase the cost of one catalog mailed to $2.00 because data-driven printing is more expensive than static printing.

Table 8.6 *Results from hypothetical static and customized catalog campaigns*

	STATIC	CUSTOMIZED
Response rate	2%	5%
Average number of new orders per year per customer	1.8	1.8
Size of order	$450	$450
Cost of goods sold as a percentage of list price	70%	70%
Cost of designing, printing, and mailing each catalog	$0.80	$2.00
Discount rate	0.12	0.12

Using the traditional direct marketing metrics, the CPR for the customized catalog campaign remains at $40.00 ($2,000,000 to mail the catalogs / 50,000 responses), but the RPM has risen to 90 (5% x 1,000 x 1.8). In other words, while the CPR and LTV values remain the same during the first year, the number of orders has substantially increased. As shown in the right-hand column of Table 8.7, the new campaign will yield a NPV profit of just over $9 million. When compared to the results from the static catalog campaign, customization is expected to produce a larger total profit.

Table 8.7 *One-year LTV calculation of hypothetical static and customized catalog campaigns*

	STATIC/MAIL MERGE CATALOG, YEAR 1	CUSTOMIZED CATALOG, YEAR 1
CUSTOMER DATA		
# of mailings	1,000,000	1,000,000
Response rate	2.0%	5.0%
# of customers who ordered	20,000	50,000
# orders/year (average)	1.8	1.8
REVENUE DATA		
Average order size	$450	$450
Total revenue per year	$16,200,000	$40,500,000
Cost of goods sold (70% of list price)	$11,340,000	$28,350,000
Net revenue	$4,860,000	$12,150,000
MARKETING COSTS		
Cost per mailing (printing and postage)	$0.80	$2.00
Total marketing cost	$800,000	$2,000,000
PROFIT		
Net profit	$4,060,000	$10,150,000
Discount rate	1.12	1.12
NPV profit	$3,625,000	$9,062,500
AVG. CUSTOMER LTV (FOR CUSTOMERS WHO ORDERED IN YEAR 1)	**$181.25**	**$181.25**
	($3,625,000/20,000)	($9,062,500/50,000)

Most business managers would quickly choose the campaign that generated $9 million as opposed to a plan that generated $3.6 million. The simple direct marketing metric of RPM might also lead them to the same conclusion.

The LTV calculations will add insight to the effectiveness of each campaign over time because LTV assesses the future impact of an original customer group. For the static catalog, if we assume that 60% of the customer group continues buying but makes fewer purchases every year, then after four years, 4,320 of the original 20,000 would remain as "active buyers." The LTV of each of these customers would be $337.

But the customized catalog campaign will give us different numbers, since personalization efforts usually pay off with a higher retention rate over time and an increase in the average number of orders per year. As shown in Table 8.8, after four years, an estimated 16,800 of the original 50,000 customers would remain "active buyers" in the sports division of Great Northern. The LTV of each of these customers would be $465.

Table 8.8 *Four-year LTV calculation for hypothetical fully customized catalog campaign*

	YEAR 1	YEAR 2	YEAR 3	YEAR 4
CUSTOMER DATA				
Retention rate		60%	70%	80%
# of customers	50,000	30,000	21,000	16,800
# orders per year	1.8	2	2.2	2.4
REVENUE DATA				
Average order	$450	$450	$450	$450
Total revenue	$40,500,000	$27,000,000	$20,790,000	$18,144,000
Cost of goods sold (70% of list)	$28,350,000	$18,900,000	$14,553,000	$12,700,800
Net revenue	$12,150,000	$8,100,000	$6,237,000	$5,443,200
MARKETING DATA				
Cost per mailing	$2.00	$2.00	$2.00	$2.00
Total marketing cost	$2,000,000	$100,000	$60,000	$42,000
PROFIT				
Net profit	$10,150,000	$8,000,000	$6,177,000	$5,401,200
Discount rate	1.12	1.25	1.40	1.57
NPV profit	$9,062,500	$6,377,551	$4,396,667	$3,432,560
Cumulative NPV profit	$9,062,500	$15,440,051	$19,836,718	$23,269,278
AVG. CUSTOMER LTV	**$181.25**	**$308.80**	**$396.73**	**$465.39**

In theory (that is, if you accept all of these assumptions), the investment in customized marketing communications pays off both in the short run, as demonstrated by RPM, and in the long run as demonstrated by LTV. Figure 8.2 shows the improving gains year-by-year in the LTV of the customized offer.

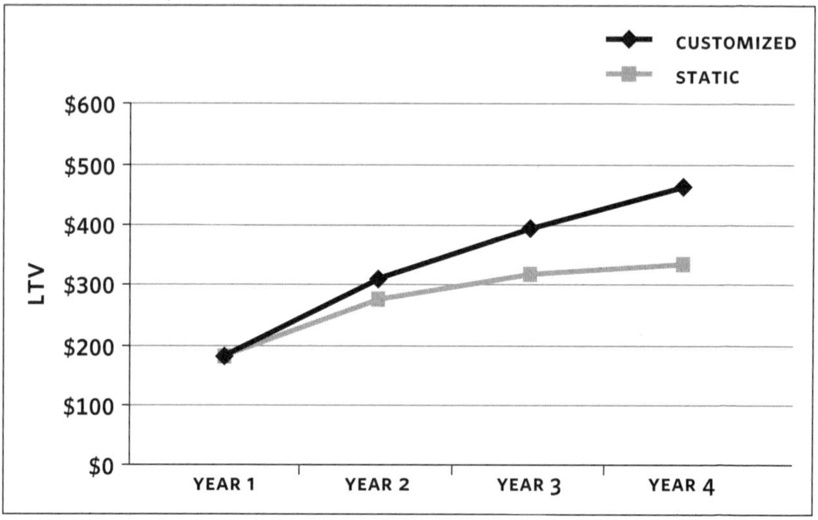

Figure 8.2 *Four-year LTV calculation of static versus customized catalog campaigns*

The marketing metrics we have discussed are extremely useful in assessing the impact of promotional tactics on sales and profits. And as we have also seen, demonstrating the effects of customized marketing communications is necessary for any business considering whether to implement such a program.

But as demonstrated in the previous section, computing an LTV for customers implies that a firm can estimate the impact of a data-driven marketing program to the bottom line over time. How many firms actually measure this? In research conducted by the Printing Industry Center on measures of effectiveness, just over one-third of marketing executives said that they "always" measured customer retention.[134] This is consistent with a 2003 Marketing Science Institute (MSI) report, where 40% of firms indicated that they used LTV measures.[135] Although this is a large proportion, it also implies that more than half of the firms do not use LTV.

CONCLUSION

To make a business case for data-driven printed communications, a print services consultant must be able to demonstrate that a customized offer will deliver more profits over time than a larger quantity of mass-produced offers. To do this, the feedback loop for marketing communications planning must be articulated at the beginning of the communications planning process. Then data must be captured and a system put in place to handle it. There are two ways to do this: outsource the whole process, or use internal resources. The nature of the firm and the products it markets will likely influence which alternative is more appropriate.

For convenience goods, where mass media advertising is the primary medium used, outsourcing the process makes sense. One drawback to this alternative is that the buying behavior of individual customers or prospects will not necessarily be evident. If a firm decides to handle its data in-house, it can also easily track individual buying behavior. While this often requires a large investment in IT infrastructure (like an enterprise-wide CRM system or campaign management system), having these resources will pay off because the firm will then be able to take advantage of customized marketing possibilities. Whether a firm decides to measure the impact of marketing efforts internally or by outsourcing methods, an orderly process for creating marketing campaign feedback systems needs to be followed.

The first step, of course, is to define the marketing objectives. Then a means through which the prospect or customer responses will be captured must be created, including how this data will be reported. This could entail setting up and staffing an 800-number, asking for specific information on a Web site, or including a postage-paid reply card on a general mailing. Who will be assigned the responsibility to track results? As we saw above, this can be outsourced to an external vendor (for example an ad agency or direct marketing firm) or be managed by an internal sales support staff. In either case, the database infrastructure that gathers the responses (in a call center, Web site, etc.) should be integrated with the marketing and fulfillment database systems, which will establish the information distribution protocols. The pertinent questions are what information needs to be reported, to whom, and how often.

In closing, in order for most resource-intensive, customized marketing communications tactics to be championed by either an internal marketing manager or an external communications consultant, the efficiency of the tactic must be demonstrated. Whether the manager or consultant uses simple direct marketing measures such as RPM, or more sophisticated LTV computations where individual consumer behavior is tracked over time, the feedback system must be a part of the initial plan.

APPENDIX 8.1: ADVERTISING EFFECTIVENESS MEASURES AND THE HIERARCHY OF EFFECTS

Advertising effectiveness metrics will vary with the objectives of a marketing campaign. Table 8.9 presents the stages of the hierarchy of advertising effects, and gives specific marketing media metrics that are commonly used at each stage.

Traditional "measured" mass media results have focused almost exclusively on the earliest stage (exposure): How many in a specified demographic audience have the *opportunity* to view the ad? This is often measured by audience composition, circulation figures, and diary methods (for example, the number of households that have a certain TV channel turned on during a specific time period). These measures are crucial only for the initial selection of the media plan.

But as media users ourselves, we know that there is a huge gap between the opportunity for exposure and whether someone actually pays attention to an advertisement. For example, the number of people who receive a newspaper on any given day is much greater than the number who read a specific advertisement in a specific edition. The number of households that have a certain TV program turned on is usually larger than the number of household members present during the airing of a particular commercial message within that program. The widespread adoption of digital video recorders and the easy availability of video and DVD movies have reduced the amount of broadcast television that households watch.

In order to measure the impact of advertising on the awareness stage of the hierarchy of advertising effects, primary research must be conducted with a target audience. Individuals who have had an opportunity to view an advertisement must be contacted directly to inquire about their recollection of it. There are a number of syndicated services that do this. Roper Starch Worldwide measures whether a consumer "noted" an ad in a magazine. Burke Advertising telephones households and tracks day-after recall for TV ads, providing reliable estimates of customer awareness of specific brands. Large firms realize that Burke's costly services are usually worth the expense. A large packaged goods firm, for example, that spends $10 million in television advertising for a new brand, would consider it a wise investment to spend $100,000 on post-advertising awareness research to assess the effectiveness of the TV ad.

Table 8.9 *Correlating the hierarchy of advertising effects with specific marketing metrics*

STAGE IN HIERARCHY OF EFFECTS	TYPICAL MEASURE/ OBJECTIVE	SYNDICATED SERVICES AND IN-HOUSE METRICS
EXPOSURE	Measured media statistics such as: • gross rating point (GRP) • television ratings • average quarter hour listening (radio) • magazine circulation • showing (outdoor advertising) • number of pieces mailed • Web site hits	• Arbitron (radio) • Neilsen (TV) • ABC (audit bureau of circulation) • TAB (traffic audit bureau) • Standard Rate and Data Service, Inc. (SRDS) publications
AWARENESS	• unaided brand recall • aided brand recall	• Starch Ad Database for magazines • Burke Advertising (day-after recall for television ads)
INTEREST	• inquiry • sales lead • store visit	No syndicated service is available. These are usually measured by: • calls to 800 number • Web site hits • reply cards returned • store traffic
PREFERENCE	• brand attitude/preference and purchase intent • brand value	• Gallup and Robinson tracking services correlate ad exposure to brand attitude and purchase intent • Interbrand brand valuation studies (global top 100 brands)
PURCHASE	• request for proposal (industrial products) • trial or initial purchase (new products) • sales using scanner data at point of sale (for mature consumer products) • orders (industrial products) • catalog orders	Test market services offered by coupon redemption services: • IOS • Coupons, Inc. • JPS In-house measures of sales: connect the purchase of an individual to a specific promotional activity (e.g., catalog version number from customer ID#)
REPURCHASE	Loyalty	An in-house measure of customer retention over time

The preference stage also requires primary research for assessment. Here the key metric determines whether targeted consumers' attitudes towards a brand have changed after an advertising campaign has been completed. The primary measure is attitude change over time. The Gallup-Robinson organization has provided this service for over 50 years.

Assessing the impact of advertising on the purchasing stage is the communications goal of many marketing campaigns for convenience products such as those found in grocery or drug stores. In most of these product categories, consumers are already aware of leading brands. In order to grow the brand, a firm must attract its competitor's customers. This is often accomplished by a price promotion. Coupon redemption programs have been a popular option for firms that distribute through retail channels. In addition, test marketing and simulated test marketing can provide realistic information on purchases of new product introductions.[136]

For B2B firms, the impact on sales is measured internally. This direct response to advertising can be tracked by customer calls to the firm's 800 number, or by tabulating reply cards or Web site logons. The firms will not only find out the number of prospects that the advertising attracted, but who they are.

How often are firms using any of the measures presented in this chapter? Printing Industry Center researchers wanted to address this issue and so asked marketing executives and advertising agencies what metrics they used and who had the responsibility for tracking the effectiveness of campaigns.[137] Their results are summarized in Figure 8.3.

First, who does the record-keeping? Seventy-five percent of marketing executives said that they measured the results internally. When the same question was asked of advertising agencies, they reported that only 37% of their clients (marketing executives) measured results internally. Another 22% said that the agencies themselves tracked the results for their clients and 34% said it was a collaborative effort.

While this may seem inconsistent (37% of ad agencies say that marketing executives measure campaign results, while 75% of marketing executives say that they themselves measure the results), recall from Chapter 3 that only half of the marketing executives we surveyed reported using advertising agencies in the previous year. In this context, if you combine the 37% estimate provided by the ad agencies and also assume that 100% of the marketing executives who did not use an agency measured their own results, the average yields a 68.5% estimate. This is likely within the margin of error provided by the 75% estimate of the marketing executive sample.

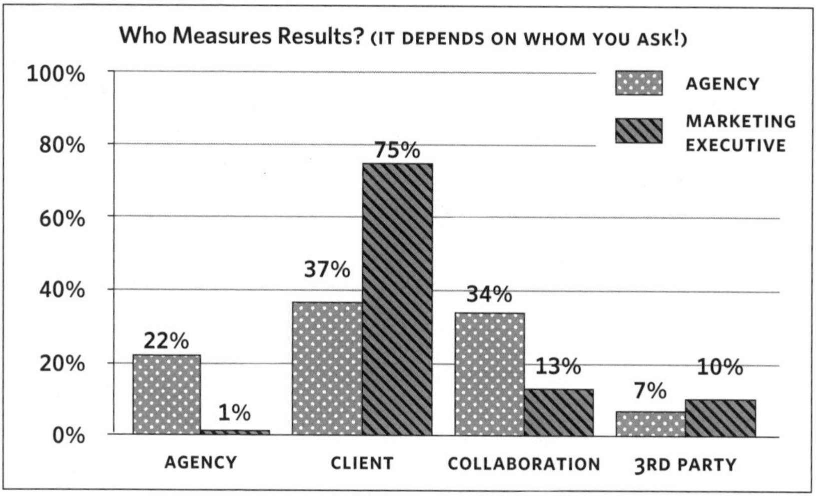

Figure 8.3 *Determining the outcomes of a marketing campaign*[138]

Both groups were also asked what specific metrics they used (see Table 8.10). Marketing executives indicated a higher use than ad agencies of almost all methods, with the exception of post-advertising awareness. Sales leads (used by 50%), a change in sales (49%), number of orders (46%), and response to direct mail (47%), were used most frequently by the marketing executives.

Table 8.10 *How success in a marketing campaign is measured*[139]

FACTORS FOR MEASURING RESULTS OF A MARKETING CAMPAIGN	PERCENT INDICATING "ALWAYS"	
	ADVERTISING AGENCIES	MARKETING EXECUTIVES
CHANGE IN SALES (BEFORE/AFTER MEASURE)	29%	49%
SALES LEADS	23%	50%
RESPONSE RATE TO DIRECT MAIL	22%	47%
POST-ADVERTISING AWARENESS	19%	11%
CUSTOMER RETENTION	12%	34%
CHANGE IN NUMBER OF CALLS TO AN 800 NUMBER	10%	15%
CHANGE IN HITS TO A WEB SITE	10%	25%
NUMBER OF ORDERS PLACED	6%	46%
RETAIL TRAFFIC/STORE COUNTS	6%	12%
ROI	6%	N/A

Arranging these results within the advertising hierarchy of effects framework, "interest" and "purchase" metrics are used more by marketing managers than by ad agencies (see Table 8.11). On the other hand, ad agencies use more post-advertising awareness measures than marketers.

Table 8.11 *Relating campaign results measures to the advertising hierarchy of effects*

STAGE IN HIERARCHY OF EFFECTS	MEASURES	AD AGENCY	MARKETING EXECUTIVE
EXPOSURE	N/A		
AWARENESS	Post-advertising awareness	19%	11%
INTEREST	Sales leads	23%	50%
	800 Number calls	10%	15%
	Web site hits	10%	25%
	Retail traffic	6%	12%
	Response rate to direct mail	22%	47%
PREFERENCE	N/A		
PURCHASE ACTION	Number of orders placed	6%	46%
REPURCHASE	Customer retention	12%	34%

As noted earlier and confirmed above, firms use multiple metrics to assess the impact of their marketing programs. If we compute how many marketing executives used direct marketing feedback methods to assess their outcomes, we find that 78% of them did. This implies that over three-fourths of the firms we surveyed had the capability to tie a specific purchase or inquiry to a specific promotional event. (For example, a $129 order was placed by customer Carol Little on January 3, 2005, from catalog # R345600-C3.)

In conclusion, though many firms use some method of assessing the impact of their marketing programs, most of the metrics are simpler than the LTV approach recommended by the authors.

122. PIMS (Profit Impact of Market Strategy) Web site, *http://www.pimsonline.com.*
123. Barwise and Farley, "Which Marketing Metrics Are Used and Where?" *http://www.msi.org/msi/publication_summary.cfm?publication=649.*
124. Winer, "What Marketing Metrics Are Used by MSI Members?" *http://www.msi.org/msi/publication_summary.cfm?publication=21.*
125. Wyner, "The ROI Toolkit."
126. Duffy, "Kraft's Return on Marketing Investment."
127. Brady, Kiley, and bureau reports, "Making Marketing Measure Up." and Beirne and Hein, "Marketer's Mantra: It's ROI or I'm Fired!"
128. McGuire, "An Information Processing Approach to Advertising Effectiveness."
129. Weilbacher, "Point of View."
130. Schultz, "Determine Outcomes First to Measure Efforts."
131. Adapted from McGuire, "An Information Processing Approach to Advertising Effectiveness."
132. Nash, *The Direct Marketing Handbook.*
133. Hughes, *Strategic Database Marketing.*
134. Sorce and Pellow, *Demand for Customized Communications by Advertising Agencies and Marketing Executives* (PICRM-2003-08).
135. Barwise and Farley, "Which Marketing Metrics Are Used and Where?" *http://www.msi.org/msi/publication_summary.cfm?publication=649.*
136. Clancy, Shulman, and Wolf, *Simulated Test Marketing.*
137. Sorce and Pellow, *Demand for Customized Communications by Advertising Agencies and Marketing Executives* (PICRM-2003-08).
138. Ibid.
139. Ibid.

CHAPTER NINE

THE INTELLIGENT USE OF DATA-DRIVEN PRINT

THE PURPOSE OF THIS BOOK is to help marketers, advertising agencies, direct marketing firms, and print services providers create promotional materials that are welcomed by the receiver. We have identified these steps to create effective marketing campaigns:

1. Fit the customized marketing communications to the business strategy.
2. Grow or acquire customer knowledge in order to customize messages.
3. Develop a creative campaign (which often includes market tests).
4. Implement the campaign.
5. Assess its effectiveness.

To get started, a firm should begin with simple levels of customization. With subsequent organizational learning about customers through data capture and analysis, more creative data-driven approaches can be designed as a result of insights gathered through data mining. Finally the success of the communications should be tracked. If the LTV metric is used and validated, it can also help the firm complete "what if" scenarios in planning for future marketing investments. These data will then provide a solid business case for incremental investments.

But for firms that are trying to determine whether they should initiate a customized program, there is a bit of a chicken-and-egg challenge: How can you show the effectiveness of data-driven print (in order to get the commitment of upper management to invest in it) if you have never conducted such a campaign? Many marketing executives use experienced communications consultants such as advertising agencies or direct marketing firms to convince top management that these programs are likely to be successful.

The critical issue to demonstrate is whether this tactic will enable a firm to achieve its business objectives. Will the investment in time and money pay off, and will the opportunity costs be worth the trouble?

The purpose of this final chapter is to address the likely questions that top management will ask of communications consultants who want to sell customized direct mail to a firm that has never used it before. First, can the communications consultant demonstrate unequivocally that customized direct mail programs will improve the bottom line? Second, will these programs grow long-term customer value? Let's examine the evidence in the public domain.

EVIDENCE FOR THE ASSUMPTIONS

First, has it been proven that response rates go up when a company starts advertising with customized marketing communications? Yes. The most convincing research regarding the difference between customized and static mailings comes from studies that use experimental methods (that is, that include both experimental and control groups). In a 2004 report from PIA/GATF's Digital Printing Council (DPC), the response rate for customized color direct mail campaigns ranged from 6% to 75%, with an average of 21%.[140] The response rates were, on average, 5.6 times higher for customized color versions than for simple mail merge applications. For example, a German utility firm mailed a customized brochure to one sample of customers and a generic brochure to a second sample. In both mailings, the brochure described the benefits of a new energy savings program, but the customized brochure included the estimated energy savings for each household based on its own particular history of energy use. The average inquiry rate for the personalized brochure was 6.3%, versus only 2.4% for the generic brochure. The customized, data-driven mailing delivered a significantly higher response rate than the generic one.

Evidence of customized marketing communications building customer loyalty is harder to find. Numerous anecdotes and case studies have been reported by business consultants who tout the pay-off for investing in loyalty programs.[141] But the real question for communications consultants who are trying to sell customized print communications is this: Can marketers build loyalty by using technology-mediated communications instead of personal interactions? As discussed in Chapter 4, loyalty and relationship marketing programs are usually built on the foundations of B2B exchanges that rely on frequent face-to-face communications. In the retail sector, interpersonal communications are also at the heart of what many consumers include in their definitions of "relationship."[142] Can we build relationships and loyalty with data-driven printed communications instead of these face-to-face communications? Or will the "junk mail" image of direct mail communications continue to haunt this most recent embodiment?

One 2001 study gives direct marketers some hope that customized marketing communications can be used to build relationships. De Wulf, Odekerken-Schröder, and Iacobucci investigated whether relationship marketing tactics used by retailers would impact the degree to which consumers would perceive that a firm was "investing" in the relationship.[143] They wondered whether the perception of an improved relationship investment (as evidenced by higher relationship quality perceptions) would lead to increased feelings of loyalty and repeat purchases. Using food and clothing retailers in both Europe and the U.S., the researchers assessed the impact of four marketing tactics:

- direct mail,
- interpersonal communication,
- preferential treatment, and
- tangible rewards.

Interpersonal communication had the largest impact of the four tactics on building relationship quality perceptions. This was the case for both societies. Direct mail also contributed to the perceptions of higher relationship quality, *but only for the European customers.* That is, direct mail did not improve perceptions of relationship quality for U.S. customers.[144]

However, there were differences among U.S. customers in their perceptions of relationship quality, and in their repeat buying patterns, according to their degrees of product involvement and "relationship proneness." That is, those who were more involved with a product and who were more likely to acknowledge that they had a relationship with a commercial entity reported higher perceived relationship quality from direct mail tactics. While this may suggest that customized marketing communications can contribute to building loyalty and LTV, these are the conclusions of just one study. Clearly, there is a need for more research in the area.

If the results of this study are validated with similar findings, it would suggest that in order for firms to build customer relationships using data-driven communications, they must first understand the attitudes that customers have towards them. As we saw in Chapter 4, firms must create a dialogue with customers to understand their preferences regarding how they want to be treated by commercial entities.

OTHER APPLICATIONS FOR DATA-DRIVEN PRINT

While the marketing and advertising world awaits the outcome of additional research, marketers can think broadly about the value of a variety of data-driven communications options. Building connections with customers extends beyond the social exchange notions of forming a relationship. Market researchers Rust, Zeithaml, and Lemon view *customer equity* as the basis for a new strategic framework from which to build customer-centered programs that are financially accountable.[145] They define a firm's customer equity as the sum of the discounted LTV of all its customers, and describe three ways to build it:

- value equity,
- brand equity, and
- retention equity.[146]

Customized marketing communications can be an effective tactic in all three routes to building customer equity. Table 9.1 shows how customized marketing communications can be applied in each case.

Table 9.1 *Three ways to build customer equity*[147]

EQUITY TYPE	DEFINITION	CUSTOMIZED COMMUNICATION GOAL
VALUE	A customer's objective assessment of the utility of a brand, driven by the product's quality, price, and convenience.	Right time, right place, right offer that leads to preference
BRAND	A customer's subjective and intangible assessment of a brand built through image and meaning. This assessment is influenced by brand awareness and "corporate citizenship."	Build a depth of knowledge in customers about the firm's brands that leads to commitment
RETENTION	Tendency of the customer to "stick with" a brand above and beyond the objective and subjective assessments.	Repeat buying and retention

In order for *value* equity to accrue, the customer must regard the firm's offering as the best value among all competitive offers. A customer who holds this view will continue to buy from the firm as long as its brand continues to deliver the best value. Simple data-driven print programs can reinforce this customer assessment. Tactics such as reminder postcards serve this function well. As we saw in Chapter 6, a customer who was reminded by a car dealer's auto service center to take care of some routine car maintenance might otherwise have neglected to call for service. If the message is timely and helps the consumer keep track of annoying responsibilities, then it delivers value and contributes to the perceived superiority of one brand over another.

To build *brand* equity, the business goal is to create an emotional connection between the customer and the brand. This approach works for high-involvement and lifestyle products. For example, some automobile manufacturers create customized publications for their customers. (See Appendix 9.1 on custom publishing at the end of this chapter.) As an Audi owner, one of our authors gets an Audi magazine once a year. It is not available on the newsstand and nor did she subscribe to it. The slick, expensive-looking magazine arrives at her home because Audi believes that most luxury or performance car owners have an emotional connection to their cars. Audi tries to bolster this connection with articles about Audi engineers, car races that Audis have won, and the exotic and beautiful vacation spots they can tour in their Audis. High-involvement products, or those that entail a significant financial or social risk, attract the type of consumers who will develop emotional attachments that can be fueled with more information. These consumers will repurchase the same or similar products because of their affective connection to the brand or manufacturer. In these best-case scenarios, a consumer's commitment to brand is so complete that alternative options are not considered.

Many brand-building efforts also have an elaborate Internet community presence that promotes interactivity. For example, the Jeep community hangs out at *http://www.jeep.com/jeep_life/index.html*. Some manufacturers sponsor special events to reinforce the community presence, like the 37 or so yearly *Jeep Jamboree* three-day weekend events at various locations across the U.S. (more in Canada). In 2005 these included an off-road training program, a women's-only event at Lake Tahoe, and a "trail adventure" in Rubicon, CA. On the company Web site's "Jamboree Lore" page, we are told that "The first Jeep Jamboree [in 1952!] saw 155 people take on the Rubicon Trail."

All of this interactivity comes at a price. Maintaining a Web presence may be expensive (never mind planning and staffing Jamboree events), but the service expectations of these loyal customers are also very high. These brand "fans" expect immediate responses to inquiries, whether they are questions about new features, reports of problems with the product, or simply account or balance information requests. Firms that pursue the route to customer equity must invest in an information infrastructure that is enterprise-wide, connecting every customer *touch point* within the firm. Though customized printed communications may not be the primary vehicle for brand building, they do play an important support role. The only limitation to leveraging the customer data accumulated by CRM activities is the creativity of the marketing or brand manager.

The third route to customer equity is *retention* equity. The continued patronage of customers may result from inertia (as in the repeat purchasing of convenience products) or the desire for rewards or savings (as in frequent flyer programs). Saving on everyday items is valued by grocery store shoppers, and is delivered when a "frequent buyer card" is scanned at the point of purchase. Though an enormous amount of data is gathered by retailers using these programs, few of them apply it to direct, data-driven communications with customers because of the privacy concerns of shoppers.

When the cost of switching to another product or service provider is high, most customers will, again because of inertia, repurchase from the same provider. Rewards and preferential treatment provide incentives to maintain a customer's continued patronage. These are often delivered by mail, perhaps on or with a monthly statement, to encourage customers to cash in on their "preferred status" through additional patronage. The preferential treatment program for Harrah's casino patrons we discussed in Chapter 4 not only made Harrah's the logical choice for repeat business, but also bestowed special privileges and recognition on patrons when they did return. These retention tactics are easily copied by competitors. It is not unusual for business travelers, for example, to have multiple frequent flyer cards.

All of these examples suggest that many firms can use customized print communications to achieve a variety of marketing goals. Regardless of the marketing strategy, data-driven print can be a vital way to build connections with customers. However as customized direct mail becomes more common, the attention-getting pull of simple forms of personalization may diminish. For the future growth of this medium, insights from data mining must be combined with creative marketing messages to ensure success. Thorough customer knowledge will be required to render customized print an effective marketing tool. The steps and strategies presented in this book will help print services providers consult with their clients in capturing and creatively using customer information to fulfill the promise of data-driven print.

APPENDIX 9.1: CUSTOM PUBLISHING

Custom publishing is not a new phenomenon. John Deere first published the magazine *Furrow* for farmers and ranchers in 1895.[148] It is still in circulation today, connecting the equipment manufacturer with its dealers and helping them deliver more value to their own local customers. The magazine's circulation peaked at 5 million in the early part of the 20th century, and now has a circulation of 1.6 million. It is customized by geographic area, with 31 regional editions.

Corporations are waking up to this medium. According to the trade group American Business Media, there are approximately 50,000 customized publications produced annually in the U.S.[149] Newsletters comprise the most popular category at 53%, and 24% are customized magazines. E-publications are growing at a fast rate and now comprise 17% of the overall annual production. Corporations spend nearly $20 million annually to print and distribute these vehicles. Not only do they provide a means for firms to connect to their customers, these publications also advertise products. The revenue stream these publications generate can offset their own printing and distribution costs.

A great example is *Menu*, a magazine published by Wegmans Food Markets in Rochester, NY.[150] *Menu* was started five years ago and comes out four times per year. The magazine's goal is clearly stated on its cover: "Helping you make great meals easy." In addition to menus and food preparation techniques, the magazine features stories about Wegmans' executive chefs, many of whom are Culinary Institute of America graduates who travel the world to find the ingredients and meal ideas that Wegmans shoppers want. Because the focus is on these in-depth feature stories, the ratio of editorial content to advertising is low.

Of the hundreds of thousands of copies that are printed, over half are mailed to a selection of "Wegmans Shopper's Club" members. The remaining copies are placed in stores and are available to shoppers at a $4.00 cover price. The magazine is designed internally and printing is outsourced to a major commercial printer. The contents of the magazine, including all recipes, are also featured on the company's Web site. Former customers who have moved out of the Northeast (where Wegmans Food Markets are located) can also order current copies or back issues of *Menu* on the site.

Judging by customer feedback gathered by the company's consumer affairs office, periodic satisfaction surveys, and the increase in the sales of featured items in the magazine, *Menu* has successfully connected grocery shoppers to the Wegmans brand. The content is not customized for individuals, but the magazine is nevertheless a good example of a printed publication targeted to a firm's high-value customers for the purpose of strengthening its bond with them.

ENDNOTES FOR CHAPTER 9

140. INTERQUEST, "Variable Data Imaging Opportunities with Digital Printing Presses."
141. Reichheld, *The Loyalty Effect.*
142. Sorce and Edwards, "Defining Business-to-Consumer Relationships."
143. De Wulf, Odekerken-Schröder, and Iacobucci, "Investments in Consumer Relationships."
144. See Dash, "Europe Zips Lips; U.S. Sells ZIPs," for a discussion of how privacy and information concerns differ between the U.S. and Europe.
145. Clancy, "Customer Equity," *http://www.copernicusmarketing.com/about/docs/customer_equity.htm.*
146. Rust, Zeithaml, and Lemon, *Driving Customer Equity.*
147. Ibid.
148. John Deere Web site, Publications, *http://johndeere.com/en_US/compinfo/publications/index.html.*
149. Publishing & Media Group, *Custom Publishing: Opportunities Abound for B-2-B Publishers, http://www.americanbusinessmedia.com/images/abm/pdfs/committees/oppb2bpubs2003.PDF.*
150. Hawkes, interview with the author.

REFERENCES

Adobe Systems, Inc. "Printing Glossary." On Adobe PostScript 3 page of Adobe Web site. http://*www.adobe.com/products/postscript/glossary.html* (accessed October 8, 2005).

American Marketing Association. "2004 Marketing Fact Book." *Marketing News* 38, no. 12: 10–22.

American Society of Magazine Editors. "Number of Magazine Titles, 1988-2004." *Editorial Trends & Magazine Handbook. http://www.magazine.org/Editorial/editorial_trends_and_magazine_handbook/1093.cfm* (accessed October 7, 2005).

Anonymous. "Planning the Next Step." *Mediaweek* 13, no. 9 (March 3, 2003): M12–13.

Bagozzi, R. P. "Toward a Formal Theory of Marketing Exchange." In *Conceptual and Theoretical Developments in Marketing*, edited by O. C. Ferrell, Stephen W. Brown, and Charles W. Lamb, Jr. Chicago, IL: American Marketing Association, 1979: 431–47.

Barwise, Patrick, and John U. Farley. "Which Marketing Metrics Are Used and Where?" *2003 MSI Reports* (Marketing Science Institute). Report no. 03-111, 2003. *http://www.msi.org/msi/publication_summary.cfm?publication=649* (accessed October 12, 2005).

Beirne, Mike, and Kenneth Hein. "Marketers' Mantra: It's ROI, or I'm Fired!" *Brandweek* 45, no. 37 (December 13, 2004): 14–15.

Brady, Diane, David Kiley, and bureau reports. "Making Marketing Measure Up: The Pressure Is On to Take the Guesswork Out of Ad Spending." *Business Week* 3912 (December 13, 2004): 112.

Campanelli, Melissa. "Ace Hardware Insert Test Passes with Flying Colors." *DM News, the Online Newspaper of Record for Direct Marketers* 26, no. 43 (November 15, 2004).

———. "Credit Card Solicitations at Highest in '04." *DM News: The Online Newspaper of Record for Direct Marketers* 27, no. 12 (March 28, 2005): 6.

Cappo, Joe. *The Future of Advertising*. Chicago: McGraw Hill, 2003.

Chakraborty, Goutam, Vishal Lala, and David Warren. "What Do Customers Consider Important in B2B Websites?" *Journal of Advertising Research* 43, no. 1 (March 2003): 50–61.

Clancy, Kevin J. "Customer Equity: A Fix for Modern Marketing." *News Room,* Copernicus Marketing Consulting, February 20, 2001. *http://www.copernicusmarketing.com/about/docs/customer_equity.htm* (accessed on October 8, 2005).

Clancy, Kevin J., Robert S. Shulman and Marianne M. Wolf. *Simulated Test Marketing: Technology for Launching Successful New Products*. New York: Lexington Books, 1994.

Cost, Frank. "Merlin International, A Case Study." Prepared for inclusion in this book. Rochester, NY, May 2005.

Cost, Frank J., and Brett J. Daly. *Digital Integration and the Lean Manufacturing Practices of U.S. Printing Firms* (PICRM-2003-09). Rochester, NY: Rochester Institute of Technology, Printing Industry Center, October 2003.

Coviello, Nicole E., Roderick J. Brodie, Peter J. Danaher, and Wesley J. Johnston. "How Firms Relate to their Markets: An Empirical Examination of Contemporary Marketing Practices." *Journal of Marketing* 66, no. 3 (July 2002): 33–47.

Creo Web site. *http://www.creopod.com.*

Dash, Eric. "Europe Zips Lips; U.S. Sells Zips." *New York Times,* August 7, 2005, Section 4: 1.

Davis, Ron H. "Printers, Payroll, and Profitability: How Profit Leaders Profit from People." *Management Portfolio*, a publication of the Printing Industries of America / Graphic Arts Technical Foundation (PIA/GATF) 1, no. 5 (September/October 2004): 22–23.

De Marco, Donna. "What's in a Name?—Online Privacy Issues and Retail Industry, United States." *Insight on the News*, July 30, 2001. *http://www.findarticles.com/p/articles/mi_m1571/is_28_17/ai_76997835* (accessed October 7, 2005).

De Wulf, Kristof, Gaby Odekerken-Schröder, and Dawn Iacobucci. "Investments in Consumer Relationships: A Cross-Country and Cross-Industry Exploration." *Journal of Marketing* 65, no. 4 (October 2001): 33–50.

Direct Marketing Association, The. Personal communication with manager of Mail Preference Services. May 2005.

———. *The State of Postal and E-Mail Marketing: New Trends and Results.* New York: Direct Marketing Assciation, 2002. *http://www.the-dma.org/research/*

———. *The DMA 2004 Response Rate Study*. New York: Direct Marketing Association, 2005. *http://www.the-dma.org/research/*

———. "*Vertical Market Trends in Direct Mail and the Impact on Production Service Providers.*" *DMA Quarterly Business Review*, October 2004. *http://www.the-dma.org/research/*

DoubleClick. *DoubleClick Spring 2002 Marketing Spending Index*. DoubleClick, Inc., June 2002. Summarized at *http://banners.noticiasdot.com/termometro/boletines/docs/consultoras/doubleclick/2002/Doubleclick_estudio_2002_ingles.pdf* (accessed October 7, 2005).

Drozdenko, Ronald G., and Perry D. Drake. *Optimal Database Marketing*. Thousand Oaks, CA: Sage Publications, Inc., 2002.

Duffy, Michael D. "Kraft's Return on Marketing Investment: Portfolio Management Planning Implications." In *Marketing Metrics*, Report No. 00-119, edited by Marion Debruyne and Katrina Hubbard. Summarized proceedings of Marketing Science Institute conference. Toronto Canada, October 5–6, 2000: 33–36.

Elkin, Tobi. "Contextual Ads Gather Steam: Marketers Target Opt-In 'Mind-Sets' Via Gator, WeatherBug, Others." *Advertising Age* 74, no. 32 (August 2003): 34.

Freeman, Steven F., and Sandra Rothenberg. *Success Under Adversity: Differentiating Leaders from Laggards During Hard Times in the Printing Industry* (PICRM-2004-10). Rochester, NY: Rochester Institute of Technology, Printing Industry Center, 2004.

Fournier, Susan, Susan Dobscha, and David Glen Mick. "Preventing the Premature Death of Relationship Marketing." *Harvard Business Review* 76, no. 1 (January/February 1998): 42–51.

Gilmore, J. H. and B. J. Pine II. "The Four Faces of Mass Customization." *Harvard Business Review* 75 (January/February 1997): 91–101.

Godin, Seth. *Permission Marketing: Turning Strangers into Friends and Friends into Customers.* New York: Simon and Schuster, 1999.

Graphic Arts Marketing Information Service (GAMIS) of Printing Industries of America (PIA). *Media Planning and Print Selection.* Sewickley, PA: Printing Industries of America, 2001.

Hawkes, John, editor of *Menu* magazine, a publication of Wegmans Food Markets. Interview with the author. Rochester, NY, May 2005.

HP Yours Truly Designer User Guide 6.5, 2004.

Hughes, Arthur M. *Strategic Database Marketing: The Masterplan for Starting and Managing a Profitable Customer-Based Marketing Program.* 2nd ed. New York: McGraw-Hill, 2000.

Iacobucci, Dawn, and Jonathan D. Hibbard. "Toward an Encompassing Theory of Business Marketing Relationships (BMRs) and Interpersonal Commercial Relationships (ICRs): An Empirical Generalization." *Journal of Interactive Marketing* 13, no. 3 (1999): 13–33.

InfoTrends/CAP Ventures. *Production Workflow Solutions Product Compendium: Digital Personalization Application Software.* Norwell, MA: CAP Ventures, January 2003.

INTERQUEST, for the Digital Printing Council of PIA/GATF. "Opportunities in Color Variable Data Imaging." Alexandria, VA: Printing Industries of America (PIA)/Graphic Arts Technical Foundation (GATF), 2004.

Jeep Web site. *The Jeep Life: Live It. http://www.jeep.com/jeep_life/index.html* (accessed October 12, 2005).

John Deere Web site. *Publications. http://johndeere.com/en_US/compinfo/publications/index.html* (accessed October 8, 2005).

Katz, Helen E. *The Media Handbook: A Complete Guide to Advertising Media Selection, Planning, Research, and Buying.* 2nd ed. Mahwah, NJ: Lawrence Erlbaum Associates, 2003.

Kelley, Larry D., and Donald W. Jugenheimer. *Advertising Media Planning: A Brand Management Approach.* Armonk, NY: M.E. Sharpe, Inc., 2004.

Kotler, Philip. *Marketing Management.* Upper Saddle River, NJ: Prentice Hall, 2003.

Loveman, Gary. "Diamonds in the Datamine." *Harvard Business Review* 81, no. 5 (May 2003): 109–113.

Manber, Udi, Ash Patel, and John Robison. "Experience with Personalization on Yahoo!" *Communications of the ACM (Association for Computing Machinery)* 43, no. 8 (August 2000): 35–39.

McArthur, D., and T. Griffin. "A Marketing Management View of Integrated Marketing Communications." *Journal of Advertising Research* 37, no. 5 (1997): 19–26.

McGuire, William J. "An Information Processing Approach to Advertising Effectiveness." In *The Behavioral and Management Sciences in Marketing*, edited by Harry J. Davis and Alvin J. Silk. New York: Ronald Press, 1978: 156–180.

Mckeon, John. "Looming in Early '06: A $9 Billion Hit?" *Graph Expo Show Daily* (2004): 12.

Morgan, Robert M. and Shelby D. Hunt. "The Commitment-Trust Theory of Relationship Marketing." *Journal of Marketing* 58, no. 3 (July 1994): 20–38.

Morris-Lee, James. "Custom Communication: Does it Pay?" *Journal of Database Marketing & Customer Strategy Management* 10, no. 2 (December 2002): 133–138.

Nash, Edward L., ed. *The Direct Marketing Handbook*. 2nd ed. New York: McGraw-Hill, 1992.

National Cable & Telecommunications Association. "History of Cable Television." In *About the Industry*, 2005. *http://www.ncta.com/industry_overview/aboutIND.cfm?indOverviewID=58* (accessed October 7, 2005).

Neisser, U. *Cognitive Psychology*. New York: Appelton-Century Crofts, 1967.

O'Malley, L. and Caroline Tynan. "Relationship Marketing in Consumer Markets: Rhetoric or Reality?" *European Journal of Marketing* 34, no. 7 (June 2000): 797–815.

Pellow, Barbara A. "Bills Can Bring More than Just Headaches: Using Monthly Statements as Vital Communication Tools." *Digital Output Magazine*, February 2004. *http://www.digitaloutput.net/content/ContentCT.asp?P=471* (accessed October 8, 2005).

Pellow, Barbara A., and Patricia Sorce. *The Role of Value-Added Services in Successful Digital Printing* (PICRM-2003-02). Rochester, NY: Rochester Institute of Technology, Printing Industry Center, October 2003.

Pellow, Barbara A., Franziska Frey, and Patricia Sorce. *Digital Color: Where Is the Market?* (PICRM-2002-02). Rochester, NY: Rochester Institute of Technology, Printing Industry Center, September 2002.

Pellow, Barbara A., Michael J. Pletka, and Heather Banis. *Investing in Digital Color...The Bottom Line* (PICRM-2003-10). Rochester, NY: Rochester Institute of Technology, Printing Industry Center, November 2003.

Pellow, Barbara A., Patricia Sorce, Franziska Frey, and Heather Banis. *Marketing Communications Demand Creation: Marketing Executive Study* (PICRM-2003-06). Rochester, NY: Rochester Institute of Technology, Printing Industry Center, October 2003.

———. *Marketing Communications Demand Creation: Marketing Executive Study, Appencides* (PICRM-2003-06). Rochester, NY: Rochester Institute of Technology, Printing Industry Center, October 2003.

Pellow, Barbara A., Patricia Sorce, Franziska Frey, Lauren Olson, Katie Moore, and Svetlana Kirpichenko. *The Advertising Agency's Role in Marketing Communications Demand Creation* (PICRM-2003-05). Rochester, NY: Rochester Institute of Technology, Printing Industry Center, October 2003.

Peppers, Don. "Jaguar Uses Mass Marketing to Learn about Individual Customers." *Inside 1to1*, Peppers & Rogers Group, a division of Carlson Marketing Group, January 17, 2005. *http://www.1to1.com/View.aspx?DocID=28658* (accessed October 8, 2005).

Peppers, Don, and Martha Rogers. *Managing Customer Relationships: A Strategic Framework*. Hoboken, NJ: John Wiley & Sons, 2004.

PODi Web site. *http://www.podi.org.*

Postma, O.J. and M. Brokke. "Personalisation in Practice: The Proven Effects of Personalisation." *Journal of Database Marketing* 9, no. 2 (2002): 137–143.

Pressey, Andrew D. and Brian P. Mathews. "Barriers to Relationship Marketing in Consumer Retailing." *Journal of Services Marketing* 14, no. 3 (May 2000): 272–285.

Publishing & Media Group, The. *Custom Publishing: Opportunities Abound for B-2-B Publishers*. American Business Media, Brand Extension Committee, January 2003. *http://www.americanbusinessmedia.com/images/abm/pdfs/committees/oppb2bpubs2003.PDF* (accessed October 8, 2005).

Reichheld, Frederick F. *The Loyalty Effect: The Hidden Force behind Growth, Profits, and Lasting Value*. Boston: Harvard Business School Press, 1996.

Reinartz, Werner J. and V. Kumar. "The Mismanagement of Customer Loyalty." *Harvard Business Review* 80, no. 7 (July 2002): 86–94.

Riggs, Larry. "Personal Press." *Direct*, April 1, 2003. *http://directmag.com/mag/marketing_personal_press/index.html* (accessed October 7, 2005).

———. "Printing and Production: A Tight Fit." *Direct*, May 1, 2001. *http://directmag.com/mag/marketing_printing_production_tight/index.html* (accessed October 7, 2005).

Rob, P. and C. Coronel. *Database Systems: Design, Implementation and Management*, Fifth Edition. Boston, MA: Thomson Course Technology, 2002.

Rodgers, Shelly and Qimei Chen. "Post-Adoption Attitudes to Advertising on the Internet." *Journal of Advertising Research* 42, no. 5 (September/October 2002): 95–104.

Romano, Frank, and James Workman. *Variable Data Printing Software*. Sewickley, PA: Printing Industries of America / Graphic Arts Technical Foundation (PIA/GATF), 2003.

Rothenberg, Sandra. *Selling Small and Smart: The Future of the Sustainable Enterprise* (PICRM-2004-01). Rochester, NY: Rochester Institute of Technology, Printing Industry Center, December 2004.

Rust, Roland T., Valarie A. Zeimthal, and Katherine M. Lemon. *Driving Customer Equity: How Customer Lifetime Value is Reshaping Corporate Strategy*. New York: The Free Press, 2000.

Schultz, Don E. "Determine Outcomes First to Measure Efforts." *Marketing News* 37, no. 18 (September 1, 2003): 7.

Schumacher, E. F. *Small is Beautiful: Economics as if People Mattered*. New York: Harper & Row, Publishers, Inc., 1973.

Schwartz, Nelson D. "Bigger and Bigger." *Fortune* 150, no. 11 (November 29, 2004): 147–151.

Sherburne, Cary. "Spirit of Innovation Drives R and R Images to Success." Sherburne & Associates, prepared exclusively for the PIA/GATF Digital Printing Council, April 2004.

Sheth, Jagdish, and Atul Parvatiyar. "The Evolution of Relationship Marketing." *International Business Review* 4, no. 4 (December 1995): 397–418.

Six Sigma Web site. "The History of Six Sigma." iSixSigma LLC. *http://www.isixsigma.com/library/content/c020815a.asp* (accessed October 11, 2005).

Sorce, Patricia. *Relationship Marketing Strategy* (PICRM-2002-04). Rochester, NY: Rochester Institute of Technology, Printing Industry Center, September 2002.

Sorce, Patricia, and Barbara A. Pellow. "Amount and Complexity of Personalization in Marketing Campaigns." Paper presented at the 16th annual Direct Marketing Educational Foundation (DMEF) Educator's Conference, New Orleans, LA, October 2004.

———. *Demand for Customized Communications by Advertising Agencies and Marketing Executives* (PICRM 2003-08). Rochester, NY: Rochester Institute of Technology, Printing Industry Center, October 2003.

Sorce, Patricia, and Kimberly Edwards. "Defining Business-to-Consumer Relationships: The Consumer's Perspective." *Journal of Database Marketing & Customer Strategy Management* 11, no. 3 (April 2004): 255–267.

Sorce, Patricia, and Michael Pletka. *Digital Printing Success Models: Validation Study, 2004* (PICRM-2004-06). Rochester, NY: Rochester Institute of Technology, Printing Industry Center, December 2004.

Treacy, Michael, and Fred Wiersema. *The Discipline Of Market Leaders: Choose Your Customers, Narrow Your Focus, Dominate Your Market*. New York: Perseus Books, 1995.

U. S. Environmental Protection Agency (EPA). "General Overview of What's In America's Trash." *Consumer Handbook for Reducing Solid Wastes*, March 2002. *http://www.epa.gov/epaoswer/non-hw/reduce/catbook/what.htm* (accessed October 7, 2005).

U. S. Postal Service. "Lowering the Landfill Levels: Ad Mail's Environmental Impact is Small, Says New Study." *Link Online Archive*, June 15, 2004. *http://liteblue.usps.gov/news/link/2004june15_1.htm* (accessed October 7, 2005).

———. *The Household Diary Study: Mail Use & Attitudes in FY 2004*. Austin, TX:

NuStats, Contract #102590-99-B-1720, April 2005. *http://www.usps.com/householddiary/welcome_print.htm* (accessed October 6, 2005).

Van de Capelle, Jean-Pierre. *An Examination of New Product Diffusion Models* (PICRM-2004-02). Rochester, NY: Rochester Institute of Technology, Printing Industry Center, October 2004.

Wann, David. "Affluenza: Curing the Bug. Five Ways to Fight Junk Marketing." *Denver Post,* September 3, 2002 (accessed March 28, 2005, from National Newspapers database, document ID: 105338344).

Weilbacher, William M. "Point of View: Does Advertising Cause a 'Hierarchy of Effects?'" *Journal of Advertising Research* 41, no. 6 (November/December 2001): 19–26.

WhatTheyThink.com. *Print Buyers Survey on Variable Data Printing*, July 30, 2001. Web site archive, "premium content" status, at *http://www.whattheythink.com.*

Winer, Russell. "What Marketing Metrics Are Used by MSI Members?" In *Marketing Metrics,* Report No. 00-119, edited by Marion Debruyne and Katrina Hubbard. Summarized proceedings of Marketing Science Institute conference. Toronto Canada, October 5–6, 2000. *http://www.msi.org/msi/publication_summary.cfm?publication=21* (accessed October 12, 2005).

Wyner, Gordon A. "The ROI Toolkit." *Marketing Research* 16, no. 3 (Fall 2004): 6–7.

Xerox Web site. *http://www.xerox.com.*

XMPie, Inc. "About Us." *http://www.xmpie.com/index.php?id=222* (accessed October 8, 2005).

Zahay, Debra L., and Abbie Griffin. "Information Antecedents of Personalisation and Customisation in Business-to-Business Service Markets." *Journal of Database Marketing & Customer Strategy Management* 10, no. 3 (April 2003): 255–271.

ABOUT THE PRINTING INDUSTRY CENTER AT RIT

The Printing Industry Center at RIT is dedicated to the study of major business environment influences on the printing industry, precipitated by new technologies and societal changes. The Center addresses the concerns of the printing industry through educational outreach, research initiatives, and print evaluation services. The Center serves as a neutral platform for the dissemination of knowledge that can be trusted by the industry, as a place for printing companies and associations to share ideas, and as a meeting ground for building the partnerships needed to sustain growth and profitability in a rapidly changing market.

With the support of RIT, the Alfred P. Sloan Foundation, and our Industry Partners, it is our mission to continue to develop and articulate the knowledge necessary for the long-term economic health of the printing industry.

R·I·T **Printing Industry Center**
An Alfred P. Sloan Foundation Center

Printing Industry Center
Rochester Institute of Technology
55 Lomb Memorial Drive
Rochester, NY 14623
http://print.rit.edu

The research agenda of the Printing Industry Center at RIT and the publication of research findings are supported by the following organizations:

INDEX